Linear Programming

Algorithms and applications

D1320285

Linear Programming
Algorithms and applications

S. VAJDA
Visiting Professor
University of Sussex

LONDON   NEW YORK

CHAPMAN AND HALL

First published in 1981
by Chapman and Hall Ltd
11 New Fetter Lane, London EC4P 4EE

Published in the USA by
Chapman and Hall
in association with Methuen, Inc.,
733 Third Avenue, New York NY 10017

© 1981 S. Vajda
Typeset by Styleset Limited, Salisbury, Wiltshire
Printed in Great Britain at the
University Press, Cambridge

ISBN 0 412 16430 2

British Library Cataloguing in Publication Data

Vajda, Steven
Linear programming. – (Science paperbacks; 167).

1. Linear programming
I. Title   II. Series
519.7'2   T57.74   80–41232

ISBN 0–412–16430–2

Contents

Preface

This text is based on a course of about 16 hours lectures to students of mathematics, statistics, and/or operational research.

It is intended to introduce readers to the very wide range of applicability of linear programming, covering problems of management, administration, transportation and a number of other uses which are mentioned in their context.

The emphasis is on numerical algorithms, which are illustrated by examples of such modest size that the solutions can be obtained using pen and paper. It is clear that these methods, if applied to larger problems, can also be carried out on automatic (electronic) computers. Commercially available computer packages are, in fact, mainly based on algorithms explained in this book.

The author is convinced that the user of these algorithms ought to be knowledgeable about the underlying theory. Therefore this volume is not merely addressed to the practitioner, but also to the mathematician who is interested in relatively new developments in algebraic theory and in some combinatorial theory as well. The chapters on duality, and on flow in networks, are particularly directed towards this aim and they contain theorems which might not be directly relevant to methods of computation. The application of the concept of duality to the theory of games is of historical interest.

It is hoped that the figures, which illustrate the results, will be found illuminating by readers with active geometrical imagination.

The references record the sources which contributed to the foundation and to the development of the subject. However, the contents of this book are meant to be self-contained.

A further development of linear programming is the field of non-linear or more generally of mathematical programming, but this is beyond the scope of the present exposition.

The mathematics used are elementary. Of algebraic concepts we use those of vectors and matrices and of their multiplication. In one place we refer to the solution of linear homogeneous equations, dependent on their rank.

CHAPTER 1

Linear programming

To introduce our topic, we start with two examples.

Example 1.1

A manufacturer produces two types of cloth, T_1 and T_2. For a unit length of T_1 he needs 4 units of some raw material R_1, 5 units of raw material R_2, and 1 unit of raw material R_3. For a unit length of T_2 the requirements are, in the same order, 1, 3 and 2 units, respectively.

The amounts of R_1, R_2 and R_3 which are available are, respectively, 56, 105, and 56.

The manufacturer estimates that from the sale of one unit of T_1 he can make a profit of 4 (in some monetary unit), and that from the sale of one unit of T_2 his profit will be 5.

He wants to know how much of T_1 and of T_2 he should produce from the available raw material, so as to maximize his total profit. We assume that he can sell all he produces.

We shall now formulate this problem algebraically. Denote the amount of T_1 produced by x_1, and that of T_2 by x_2. He then needs $4x_1 + x_2$ of raw material R_1, and this must not exceed 56. Thus

$$4x_1 + x_2 \leqslant 56$$

Similarly, regarding R_2 and R_3

$$5x_1 + 3x_2 \leqslant 105$$

and

$$x_1 + 2x_2 \leqslant 56$$

His profit will be $4x_1 + 5x_2 = B$ (for 'benefit'), and he should choose x_1 and x_2 so as to maximize this expression, not forgetting that neither x_1 nor x_2 must be negative; explicitly

$$x_1 \geqslant 0, x_2 \geqslant 0.$$

We consider now a second problem, which is called the 'nutrition problem' in the literature of our subject.

Example 1.2
There are two types of food on the market, F_1 and F_2. They contain three different nutritional ingredients, N_1, N_2 and N_3. One unit of F_1 contains, respectively, 3, 4 and 1 units of these, and one unit of F_2 contains 1, 3 and 2 units.

A housewife has been told that she needs, for her family, 3 units of N_1, 6 of N_2, and 2 of N_3. She wants to obtain these ingredients by purchasing the available food items at the smallest total cost. One unit of F_1 costs 20, and one unit of F_2 costs 10 (in some monetary unit).

The housewife's problem can be formulated as follows, if y_1 is the amount of F_1 and y_2 that of F_2 to be bought.

Minimize

$$20y_1 + 10y_2 = C \text{ (for 'cost')}$$

subject to

$$3y_1 + y_2 \geqslant 3$$
$$4y_1 + 3y_2 \geqslant 6$$
$$y_1 + 2y_2 \geqslant 2$$
$$y_1 \geqslant 0, y_2 \geqslant 0$$

We have written the conditions as inequalities, because it might be cheaper to obtain more of some ingredient than necessary if it is contained abundantly in some other food item which supplies other ingredients as well.

The two examples which we have given are instances of *linear programming* problems. In such formulations it is required to optimize (maximize or minimize) a linear expression, the 'objective function', subject to linear inequalities, the 'constraints'.

There is no fundamental algorithmic difference between maximizing and minimizing, because max $f(x)$ equals $-\min [-f(x)]$.

In the maximizing problem the left hand side of a constraint was not larger than the right hand side (a constant), while in the minimizing problem the opposite was true. Again, there is no fundamental algebraic difference between the two cases, because if $f(x) \leqslant c$, then $-f(x) \geqslant -c$.

An inequality $a_1x_1 + \cdots + a_nx_n \leqslant c$ can be written as an equation $a_1x_1 + \cdots + a_nx_n + x_{n+1} = c$, with $x_{n+1} \geqslant 0$. We call such an additional variable a 'slack' variable. In an inequality $a_1x_1 + \cdots + a_nx_n \geqslant c$ we would subtract a non-negative slack variable from the left hand side to convert it into an equivalent equation.

Conversely, an equation $a_1x_1 + \cdots + a_nx_n = c$ can be written as a pair of two simultaneous inequalities, thus

$$a_1x_1 + \cdots + a_nx_n \leqslant c$$

and

$$-a_1x_1 - \cdots - a_nx_n \leqslant -c$$

Another way of converting the given equation, in non-negative variables, into an inequality, consists in choosing one of the a_i which is not zero, say a_n, solving for x_n, namely

$$x_n = \frac{c - a_1x_1 - \cdots - a_{n-1}x_{n-1}}{a_n} \geqslant 0$$

and writing

$$\frac{a_1x_1}{a_n} + \cdots + \frac{a_{n-1}x_{n-1}}{a_n} \leqslant \frac{c}{a_n}$$

If a variable, say x, is not required to be non-negative, then in order to keep within the usual framework we replace it by two new variables which are required to be non-negative, thus $x = x' - x''$.

We now define the term linear programming. We mean by it maximizing or minimizing a linear function of non-negative variables, subject to linear constraints (equations or inequalities).

In algebraic matrix notation we have a linear programming problem. Maximize $b'x$, subject to $Ax \leqslant c$, where A is a matrix of m rows and n columns, c is an m-vector, and x as well as b are n-vectors. The co-ordinates of x are the variables to be determined, while A, b, and c are known. The vector x is also required to have non-negative co-ordinates (transposition of a vector or of a matrix will be denoted by a prime).

If we introduce slack variables explicitly, then we have $Ax + I_m\mathbf{x} = c$, where I_m is the identity matrix of order m, and $\mathbf{x}$ is the

m-vector of slack variables. The number of all variables is then $n + m = N$, say.

In order to obtain a diagrammatic representation, we think of the components of x as ordinates of a point in a space of n dimensions. In the examples above we had $n = 2$, and we can therefore use diagrams in a plane. The diagram for Example 1.1 is Fig. 1.1. We have drawn

the x_1-axis $x_2 = 0$

the x_2-axis $x_1 = 0$

and the straight lines

$$4x_1 + x_2 = 56$$

$$5x_1 + 3x_2 = 105$$

$$x_1 + 2x_2 = 56$$

Introducing slack variables x_3, x_4, and x_5 into the inequality constraints, the last three equations can be written

$$x_3 = 0, x_4 = 0, x_5 = 0$$

Every straight line of the diagram is thus described by one of 5 variables being zero.

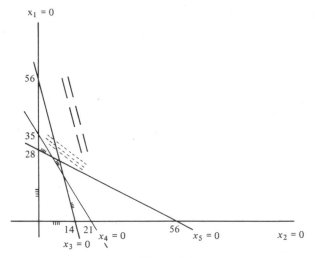

Figure 1.1

The points with $x_i \geqslant 0$ lie in a half-plane on one side of the line $x_i = 0$ or on this line. The correct side is easily ascertained by determining that half-plane in which $(0, 0)$ lies, unless this point lies on the line itself.

In the diagram we have indicated the excluded side, that on which x_i is negative, by short spikes on the lines $x_i = 0$, pointing into that half-plane. The feasible points, i.e. those whose co-ordinates satisfy all constraints, form the 'feasible region'; in the present case it is a pentagon, with vertices

$$(0, 0), (14, 0), (9, 20), (6, 25), \text{ and } (0, 28).$$

We have still to represent the requirement of maximizing $4x_1 + 5x_2$. Now the lines $4x_1 + 5x_2 = B$, with varying values of B, form a pencil of parallel straight lines, indicated in the diagram by dotted lines. We want to find that line which belongs to the largest B, with at least one point in the feasible region. It is the line through $(6,25)$ namely $4x_1 + 5x_2 = 149$.

Example 1.2 can be represented by Fig. 1.2

The feasible region is unbounded. Its vertices are

$$(2, 0), (6/5, 2/5), (3/5, 6/5), (0, 3)$$

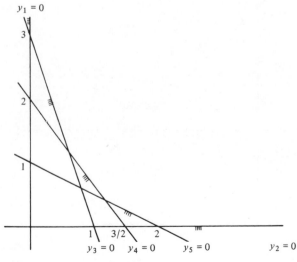

Figure 1.2

The minimum of $20y_1 + 10y_2$ in the feasible region equals 24, at $(3/5, 6/5)$.

We define now the concept of a basic feasible solution. It is a feasible solution $(x, \bar{x})$, n components of which are zero, such that the set of constraints can be solved for the remaining m components, with non-negative values. (Recall that m is the number of constraints, and that $n + m$ is the number of all variables, including slack variables.) The m variables for which we solve are called basic, those n components which are zero are non-basic variables. Of course, some of the basic variables may also be equal to zero. If this is the case, then we call the solution degenerate. For instance, take the following example.

Example 1.3

When

$$2x_1 - x_2 + x_3 = 4$$
$$x_1 - 2x_2 + x_4 = 2$$
$$x_1 + x_2 + x_5 = 5$$

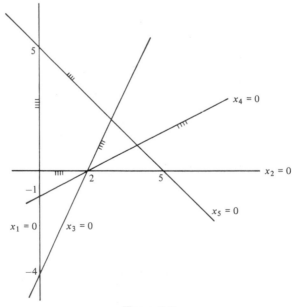

Figure 1.3

we obtain, after putting $x_2 = x_3 = 0$,

$$x_1 = 2, x_4 = 0, x_5 = 3$$

Here we have $m = 3$, $n = 2$, but in the event there are 3 variables which are zero. In the corresponding diagram (Fig. 1.3) three lines pass through the same point.

In Example 1.1, we can, for instance, put the slack variables x_4 and x_5 equal to zero, and then solve the system

$$4x_1 + x_2 + x_3 = 56$$
$$5x_1 + 3x_2 \quad\quad = 105$$
$$x_1 + 2x_2 \quad\quad = 56$$

The solution is $x_1 = 6, x_2 = 25, x_3 = 7$.

Setting other suitable pairs of components equal to zero, we obtain other feasible, basic solutions. Thus:

non-basic	basic
x_1, x_2	$x_3 = 56, x_4 = 105, x_5 = 56$
x_1, x_5	$x_2 = 28, x_3 = 28, x_4 = 21$
x_2, x_3	$x_1 = 14, x_4 = 35, x_5 = 42$
x_3, x_4	$x_1 = 9, x_2 = 20, x_5 = 7$
x_4, x_5	see example above

If we choose other variables, we do not obtain a non-negative solution. To make it clear why we stress that the set of non-basic variables chosen must be such that the remaining system can be solved, we consider Example 1.4.

Example 1.4

$$2x_1 + 4x_2 + x_3 \leqslant 4 \quad\quad \text{or} \quad\quad 2x_1 + 4x_2 + x_3 + x_4 = 4$$
$$3x_1 + 6x_2 + 4x_3 \leqslant 12 \quad\quad \text{or} \quad\quad 3x_1 + 6x_2 + 4x_3 + x_5 = 12$$

If we now set $x_3 = x_4 = x_5 = 0$, we have

$$2x_1 + 4x_2 = 4, \quad 3x_1 + 6x_2 = 12$$

and this system has no solution.

If we look at Fig. 1.4, we see the reason. The planes $x_3 = 0$, $x_4 = 0$ and $x_5 = 0$ have no point in common: the line of intersection between the first two, and the line of intersection between the first and the third, are parallel.

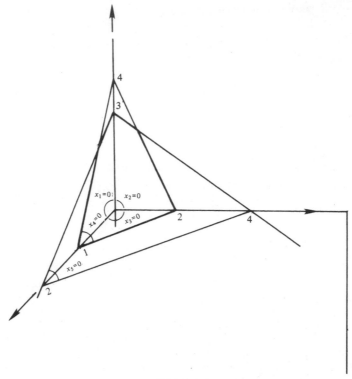

Figure 1.4

It will be noticed that the basic feasible solutions of Example 1.1 correspond to the vertices of Fig. 1.1. We shall now prove that such a correspondence between basic feasible solutions and vertices of the feasible region must always be the case.

To do this, we must first define a vertex algebraically. A vertex is a vector $(x_1, \ldots, x_m, x_{m+1}, \ldots, x_{n+m})$ with non-negative components, which does not lie half-way between any other two such vectors.

Let a basic feasible vector $P_0 = (x_1, \ldots, x_m, 0, \ldots, 0)$ be given. Any other feasible vector P_1 has co-ordinates $(y_1, \ldots, y_m, y_{m+1},$

$\ldots, y_{m+n}$). If P_0 is half-way between P_1 and some other feasible vector P_2, then $P = \frac{1}{2}(P_1 + P_2)$, or

$$P_2 = 2P_0 - P_1$$
$$= (2x_1 - y_1, \ldots, 2x_m - y_m, -y_{m+1}, \ldots, -y_{m+n})$$

Because a feasible vector has no negative components, P_2 is feasible only if $y_{m+1} = \cdots = y_{m+n} = 0$. Then $P_0 = P_1 - P_2$.

Conversely, for a feasible vector V to correspond to a vertex, m of its components must be zero, otherwise we could find P_1 and P_2 both feasible and different from V, such that $V = \frac{1}{2}(P_1 + P_2)$. It follows that a vertex corresponds to a basic feasible solution.

We prove now a few theorems which characterize the feasible region, and which show the importance of the concept of a basic feasible solution in the search for optimal solutions.

Theorem 1.1
The feasible region, formed by all points x which satisfy the constraints $Ax \leqslant c$ and $x \geqslant 0$ is (i) convex, and (ii) polyhedral.

Proof
Let $x^{(i)}$ and $x^{(ii)}$ be feasible points, i.e.

$$Ax^{(i)} \leqslant c, \; Ax^{(ii)} \leqslant c, \; x^{(i)} \geqslant 0, \; x^{(ii)} \geqslant 0$$

When

$$\lambda_1 \geqslant 0 \text{ and } \lambda_2 \geqslant 0, \text{ and } \lambda_1 + \lambda_2 = 1,$$

then

$$A[\lambda_1 x^{(i)} + \lambda_2 x^{(ii)}] \leqslant \lambda_1 c + \lambda_2 c = c$$

and

$$\lambda_1 x^{(i)} + \lambda_2 x^{(ii)} \geqslant 0$$

Thus every point on the line segment connecting $x^{(i)}$ and $x^{(ii)}$ is also feasible, so that the feasible region is convex.

The boundary of a feasible region is composed of segments of the lines $x_i = 0$ $(i = 1, \ldots, n, n+1, \ldots, n+m)$, and this is what polyhedral means.

Theorem 2
If a feasible solution exists, and the matrix of coefficients A has rank

m (the number of constraints $Ax \leqslant c$), then a basic feasible solution also exists.

Proof

Let $x_1^0 > 0, \ldots,\ x_t^0 > 0, x_{t+1}^0 = 0, \ldots, x_{n+m}^0 = 0$, and $t > m$, so that $(x_1^0, \ldots, x_{n+m}^0)$ is a feasible solution, although not a basic one.
   The matrix

$$\begin{pmatrix} a_{11} \ldots a_{1t} \\ \cdot \quad\quad \cdot \\ \cdot \quad\quad \cdot \\ \cdot \quad\quad \cdot \\ a_{m1} \ldots a_{mt} \end{pmatrix}$$

has rank $r \leqslant m < t$. Therefore we can solve the system of equations

$$\alpha(k_1 a_{11} + \cdots + k_t a_{1t}) = 0$$
$$\cdot \quad\quad\quad\quad\quad\quad \cdot$$
$$\cdot \quad\quad\quad\quad\quad\quad \cdot$$
$$\cdot \quad\quad\quad\quad\quad\quad \cdot$$
$$\alpha(k_1 a_{m1} + \cdots + k_t a_{mt}) = 0$$

with arbitrary α for $k_1, \ldots, k_t$, not all of these equal to zero. For sufficiently small $|\alpha|$ we can also find $(x_1', \ldots, x_{m+n}')$ such that

$$x_1' = x_1^0 + \alpha k_1 \geqslant 0, \ldots, x_t' = x_t^0 + \alpha k_t \geqslant 0$$

and

$$x_{t+1}' = x_{t+1}^0 = 0, \ldots, x_{n+m}' = x_{n+m}^0 = 0$$

These also form a feasible solution. We choose α so that at least one of the $x_j' (j = 1, \ldots, t)$ is also zero, and we continue in this manner until not more than m components are positive.

   If at one stage precisely m components are positive and the relevant matrix of coefficients of the k_i is non-singular, then we cannot continue but then we have reached a basic feasible solution, since that matrix is the matrix of coefficients of the corresponding variables in the constraints. If we can continue, then we obtain a feasible solution with less than m components being positive and more than n components equal to zero. This situation can also emerge from a previous state, if we make more than one additional component zero (such a case is given in Example 1.6).

Example 1.5

In Example 1.1, $x = (10, 6, 10, 37, 34)$ is a feasible solution, although of course not a basic one. Here $t = 5, m = 3$. We solve

$$4x_1 + \ k_2 + k_3 = 0$$

$$5k_1 + 3k_2 + k_4 = 0$$

$$k_1 + 2k_2 + k_5 = 0$$

One solution is, for instance

$$(k_1, k_2, k_3, k_4, k_5) = (1, 1, -5, -8, -3)$$

Then

$$x'_1 = 10 + \alpha, \ x'_2 = 6 + \alpha, \ x'_3 = 10 - 5\alpha$$

$$x'_4 = 37 - 8\alpha, \ x'_5 = 34 - 3\alpha$$

Let $\alpha = 2$, then $x' = (12, 8, 0, 21, 28)$. Now t has been reduced to 4. We solve

$$4k_1 + \ k_2 \qquad = 0$$

$$5k_1 + 3k_2 + k_4 = 0$$

$$k_1 + 2k_2 + k_5 = 0$$

$$(k_1, k_2, k_4, k_5) = (1, -4, 7, 7)$$

which produces

$$x''_1 = 12 + \alpha, x''_2 = 8 - 4\alpha, x''_3 = 0,$$

$$x''_4 = 21 + 7\alpha, x''_5 = 28 + 7\alpha$$

Now let $\alpha = 2$, and

$$x'' = (14, 0, 0, 35, 42)$$

is a basic feasible solution.

Example 1.6 (see Fig. 1.3)

Consider again the constraints of Example 1.3. A feasible solution is $(1, 1, 3, 3, 3)$. The system

$$2k_1 - \ k_2 + k_3 = 0$$

$$k_1 - 2k_2 + k_4 = 0$$

$$k_1 + \ k_2 + k_5 = 0$$

is satisfied, for instance, by

$$(k_1, k_2, k_3, k_4, k_5) = (1, -1, -3, -3, 0)$$

if we then choose $\alpha = 1$, we obtain

$$1 + k_1\alpha = 2, 1 + k_2\alpha = 0, 3 + k_3\alpha = 0$$

$$3 + k_4\alpha = 0, 3 + k_5\alpha = 3$$

$x_1 = 2$, $x_5 = 3$, with any one of the other $x_i = 0$, form a basic feasible solution.

Theorem 1.3
Unless the feasible region is unbounded, every feasible solution is a weighted combination of basic feasible solutions, with non-negative weights adding up to unity.

Proof
Consider again the procedure in the proof of Theorem 2. There we used a value of α, say α_1, to decrease (at least) one of the variables to zero. We now choose a value α_2 in order to increase that variable, until another variable becomes zero. This is certainly possible if the feasible region is bounded.

Let the original feasible solution be $(x_1^0, \ldots, x_{m+n}^0)$ If, then

$$x_j' = x_j^0 + \alpha_1 k_j \text{ and } x_j'' = x_j^0 + \alpha_2 k_j \text{ (all } j)$$

then

$$x_j^0 = (\alpha_1 x_j'' - \alpha_2 x_j')/(\alpha_1 - \alpha_2) = \frac{\alpha_1}{\alpha_1 - \alpha_2} x_j'' + \frac{\alpha_2}{-\alpha_1 + \alpha_2} x_j'$$

The weights add up to unity, and they are non-negative, because if $k_1 < 0$, then $\alpha_1 > 0$, $\alpha_2 < 0$, and if $k_2 > 0$, then $\alpha_1 < 0$, $\alpha_2 > 0$.

The two solutions x' and x'' may themselves not be basic as yet, but if we continue, x^0 will eventually be a combination of basic feasible solutions, with non-negative weights adding up to unity, as the theorem states.

Example 1.7
We start from $x^0 = (10, 6, 10, 37, 34)$, as in Example 1.5. When $\alpha = 2$, we obtain

$$x' = (12, 8, 0, 21, 28)$$

and when $\alpha = -6$, then

$$x'' = (4, 0, 40, 85, 52)$$

In this case we have $x^0 = 3x'/4 + x''/4$. However, x' and x'' are not basic. From x' we obtain, as above, with $\alpha = 2$,

$$x^{(11)} = (14, 0, 0, 35, 42)$$

or, with $\alpha = -3$,

$$x^{(12)} = (9, 20, 0, 0, 7)$$

and

$$x^{(3)} = 3x^{(11)}/5 + 2x^{(12)}/5.$$

On the other hand, from x'' we obtain, through

$$4k_1 + k_3 = 0, 5k_1 + k_4 = 0, k_1 + k_5 = 0$$

i.e.

$$k_1 = 1, k_3 = -4, k_4 = -5, k_5 = -1$$

with $\alpha = -4$,

$$x^{(21)} = (0, 0, 56, 105, 56)$$

and with $\alpha = 10$

$$x^{(22)} = (14, 0, 0, 35, 42) = x^{(11)}$$

Now

$$x'' = 5x^{(21)}/7 + 2x^{(22)}/7$$

Finally

$$x^0 = 9x^{(11)}/20 + 3x^{(12)}/10 + 5x^{(21)}/28 + x^{(22)}/14$$

Once more, the weights add up to unity.

Theorem 1.4

If an optimal solution $(x_1^0, \ldots, x_{m+n}^0)$ exists, then at least one basic optimal solution exists as well.

Proof

Let $x_1^0 > 0, \ldots x_t^0 > 0, x_{t+1}^0 = x_{t+2}^0 = \cdots = x_{n+m}^0 = 0, t > m,$ and let the optimal value of the objective function be

$$b_1 x_1^0 + \cdots + b_{n+m} x_{n+m}^0$$

Consider

$$b_1 x_1' + \cdots + b_{n+m} x_{n+m}'$$

$$= b_1 x_1^0 + \cdots + b_{n+m} x_{n+m}^0 + \alpha(b_1 k_1 + \cdots + b_t k_t)$$

where k_j has the same meaning as in earlier theorems. α is arbitrary, and therefore $b_1 x_1^0 + \cdots + b_{n+m} x_{n+m}^0$ could not be optimal if $b_1 k_1 + \cdots + b_t k_t$ were not zero. The factor α can be chosen so that one more x_j^0 equals zero, and thus we can construct a basic feasible solution which is optimal.

Theorem 1.5
Unless the feasible region is unbounded, the optimal solution is a non-negatively weighted combination of optimal basic feasible solutions, with weights adding up to unity. Every such combination is optimal (this includes the case where only one single optimal solution exists).

The proof is analogous to that of Theorem 1.3.

Theorem 1.6
A local optimum is a global optimum.

Proof
Let x^0 be a local optimum, i.e. let there be a value $\epsilon > 0$ such that

$$b_1 x_1^0 + \cdots + b_{n+m} x_{n+m}^0 > b_1 x_1' + \cdots + b_{n+m} x_{n+m}' \qquad (1.1)$$

when the distance $| x^0 - x' | \leqslant \epsilon$.

Now assume that x^0 is not a global optimum, i.e. that there is a feasible vector $x^* \neq x^0$, such that

$$b' x^* > b' x^0 \qquad (1.2)$$

(such an x^* would, of course, be outside the neighbourhood of x^0 defined by ϵ). Then

$$b'(\lambda_1 x^* + \lambda_2 x^0] > b'(\lambda_1 x^0 + \lambda_2 x^0) = b' x^0 \qquad (1.3)$$

for any $\lambda_1 \geqslant 0, \lambda_2 \geqslant 0, \lambda_1 + \lambda_2 = 1$.

But this is impossible because

$$|x^0 - (\lambda_1 x^* + \lambda_2 x^0)| = \lambda_1 |x^* - x^0|,$$

and when

$$\lambda_1 < \epsilon/|x^* - x^0|$$

then

$$|x^0 - (\lambda_1 x^* + \lambda_2 x^0)| < \epsilon$$

so that Equation (1.1) must hold for $x' = \lambda_1 x^* + \lambda_2 x^0$, which contradicts Equation (1.3).

Problem

1.1. Determine the vertices of the region of the plane defined by

$$3x_1 + 4x_2 \leqslant 18, \quad 2x_1 + x_2 \leqslant 7$$

$$x_1 \geqslant 0, \quad x_2 \geqslant 0.$$

CHAPTER 2

Algorithms

We shall now describe various algorithms for the solution of linear programming problems. We start with the *Simplex Method*, devised by Dantzig[2]. The name of this method is due to its history, and does not reflect any of its features in applications.

We write the constraints in the form of equations, using slack variables if necessary. We then try to find a 'first solution' by solving the constraints for m basic variables. This might be difficult, or even impossible, if the equations are contradictory. We shall discuss this situation later. However, if the constraints are of the form

$$Ax + \mathbf{x} = c$$

and c is non-negative, or of the form

$$Ax - \mathbf{x} = d$$

and d is non-positive, then the choice of the basic variables is obvious: they are the slack variables.

Let us consider $Ax + \mathbf{x} = c$, $c \geqslant 0$. Renumbering the subscripts, if necessary, we may assume that the slack variables are $x_{n+1}, \ldots, x_{n+m}$, and that we have constraints of the form

$$x_{n+j} + a_{j1}x_1 + a_{j2}x_2 + \cdots + a_{jn}x_n = c_j (j = 1, 2, \ldots, m)$$

In the objective function B we substitute for $x_{n+1}, \ldots, x_{n+m}$ (if they appear at all)

$$x_{n+j} = c_j - a_{j1}x_1 - \cdots \cdot a_{jn}x_n$$

so that we obtain an expression of the form

$$B = b_1 x_1 + \cdots + b_n x_n + b_0$$

We may say that the basic variables and B are expressed in terms of the non-basic variables $x_1, \ldots, x_n$.

Regarding numerical values, at this stage

$$x_1 = \cdots = x_n = 0$$

and
$$x_{n+j} = c_j (j = 1, \ldots, m)$$

We assume that the constraints were such that all c_j are positive. We shall deal, in due course, with complications which arise on this score.

It is our aim to maximize B, and to find the basic variables — or equivalently the non-basic variables — which achieve this. The non-basic variables have value zero, and no variable is allowed to have a negative value. Therefore, if one of the $b_i (i = 1, \ldots, n)$, say b_{i_0}, is positive, then it is useful to increase x_{i_0}.

The question arises how far x_{i_0} may be increased. A limit in the increase is due to the fact that no other variable is allowed to become negative as a consequence.

Assume that x_{i_0} increases to a positive value, while the other x_i remain equal to zero. Then the equations above show that
$$x_{n+j} = c_j - a_{j,i_0} x_{i_0}$$
and
$$B = b_{i_0} x_{i_0} + b_0$$

and B has indeed increased from b_0, because $b_{i_0} > 0$.

Scrutinizing $x_{n+j} (j = 1, \ldots, m)$ we find that those in which a_{j,i_0} is negative have also increased; they are in no danger of becoming negative. On the other hand, if $a_{j,i_0} > 0$, then $x_{i_0} > c_j / a_{j,i_0}$ means $x_{n+j} < 0$. Hence x_{i_0} may not be made larger than the smallest of $c_j / a_{j,i_0}$ for all j for which a_{j,i_0} is positive. This is then the limit to which we increase x_{i_0}.

If this value is obtained when $j = j_0$, then the increase of x_{i_0} to its limit makes at least one x_{n+j}, namely x_{n+j_0} equal to zero. This also means a change in the sets of basic and non-basic variables. In fact, x_{i_0} and x_{n+j_0} exchange places.

For simplicity of notation, let $i_0 = 1$, and $j_0 = 1$. Again we want to express the basic variables in terms of the non-basic ones, and algebraic re-grouping produces

$$x_1 + \frac{1}{a_{1,1}} x_{n+1} + \frac{a_{1,2}}{a_{1,1}} x_2 + \cdots + \frac{a_{1,n}}{a_{1,1}} x_n = \frac{c_1}{a_{1,1}}$$

$$x_{n+j} - \frac{a_{j,1}}{a_{1,1}} x_{n+1} + \left(a_{j,2} - \frac{a_{1,2} a_{j,1}}{a_{1,1}} \right) x_2 + \cdots$$

$$+ \left(a_{j,n} - \frac{a_{1,n} a_{j,1}}{a_{1,1}} \right) x_n = c_j - \frac{a_{j,1}}{a_{1,1}} c_1$$

and

$$B + \frac{b_1}{a_{1,1}} x_{n+1} - \left(b_2 - \frac{a_{1,2}b_1}{a_{1,1}} \right) x_2 - \cdots - \left(b_n - \frac{a_{1,n}b_1}{a_{1,1}} \right) x_n$$

$$= b_0 + \frac{b_1 c_1}{a_{1,1}}$$

We look again at the coefficients of the non-basic variables in the expression for B, and using the same criteria as before, about the possibility of further increasing the value of B, we proceed if possible.

It will be noticed that in this way we are dealing at each stage only with basic feasible solutions. In view of Theorem 1.4 in Chapter 1 we do not lose anything by thus restricting ourselves.

The following description will show how we proceed in practice if we apply this method. There are computer packages which imitate this procedure.

We illustrate the algorithm by again using Example 1.1. Instead of writing out all equations algebraically or numerically, we adopt the following tableau form.

	x_1	x_2	
B	-4	-5	0
x_3	4*	1	56
x_4	5	3	105
x_5	1	2	56

It will be clear how such a tableau is to be read. For instance, the first line reads $B - 4x_1 - 5x_2 = 0$, and the last line reads $x_5 + x_1 + 2x_2 = 56$. The labels of the rows are B, and the basic variables, those of the columns are the non-basic variables.

The value -4 in the B-row and x_1 column shows that we may profitably increase x_1. Its increase is limited by the smallest of $56/4$, $105/5$, and $56/1$, i.e. the limit is 14, and we exchange x_1 and x_3.

We have shown above the algebraic transformations which produce the next tableau. In terms of practical procedure we can express the rules of tableau transformation as follows:

1. Call the value in the row and column of the variables to be exchanged (here x_1 and x_3) the 'pivot': it is indicated by an asterisk

2. In the new tableau write, where the pivot was, its reciprocal
3. The other values in the row of the pivot are divided by the pivot
4. The remaining values in the pivotal column are divided by the negative pivot.

So far, we have obtained the following portion of the new tableau:

	x_3	x_2	
B	1		
x_1	1/4	1/4	14
x_4	−5/4		
x_5	−1/4		

5. As regards any of the remaining positions, with entry v, say, denote the value in its row and in the pivotal column by c, the value in its column and the pivotal row by r, call the pivot p and replace v by $v - rc/p$. This completes the new tableau T_1.

	x_3	x_2	
B	1	−4	56
x_1	1/4	1/4	14
x_4	−5/4	7/4*	35
x_5	−1/4	7/4	42

The lines of the basic variables are transformations of the original constraints, and equivalent to them.

We have now proceeded from the solution (0, 0, 56, 105, 56) to the solution (14, 0, 0, 35, 42), but we have not yet finished because there is still a negative value in the B-row, and x_2 can be increased to min $[14/(1/4), 35/(7/4), 42/(7/4)] = 20$. The new non-basic variable is x_4.

Once more applying the rules of tableau transformation we obtain T_2

	x_3	x_4	
B	−13/7	16/7	136
x_1	3/7	−1/7	9
x_2	−5/7	4/7	20
x_5	1*	−1	7

and finally T_3

	x_5	x_4	
B	13/7	3/7	149
x_1	−3/7	2/7	6
x_2	5/7	−1/7	25
x_3	1	−1	7

Looking at Fig. 1.1, we see that we started from the origin, moved to an adjacent vertex, then to another adjacent vertex, and then to the vertex which we found to be optimal.

The result that x_3 is positive means that the raw material R_1 will not be used up completely, while nothing will be left of R_2 and of R_3.

We have been discussing the Simplex Method for a case where we want to maximize an objective function; if we wanted to minimize an objective function, then positive values in the first row of the tableau would call for changes. The rules of tableau transformation would remain the same.

We add some algebraic considerations, which lead to a check of the calculations which might sometimes be useful. Let us describe any tableau as follows, assuming, without loss of generality, that the basic variables are $x_1, \ldots, x_m$

		(b_{m+1})		(b_{m+j})		(b_{m+n})	(b_0)
		x_{m+1}	...	x_{m+j}	...	x_{m+n}	
	B	$z_{0,m+1}$	...	$z_{0,m+j}$	...	$z_{0,m+n}$	$z_{0,0}$
(b_1)	x_1	$z_{1,m+1}$	...	$z_{1,m+j}$	...	$z_{1,m+n}$	$z_{1,0}$
		.		.		.	
		.		.		.	
		.		.		.	
(b_i)	x_i	$z_{i,m+1}$	...	$z_{i,m+j}$	...	$z_{i,m+n}$	$z_{i,0}$
		.		.		.	
		.		.		.	
		.		.		.	
(b_m)	x_m	$z_{m,m+1}$	...	$z_{m,m+j}$	...	$z_{m,m+n}$	$z_{m,0}$

(we shall explain the expressions in brackets, on the left of and above labels, below).

We recall that the lines of the tableau mean

$$B = z_{0,0} - z_{0,m+1}x_{m+1} - \cdots - z_{0,m+n}x_{m+n} \qquad (2.1)$$

and

$$x_i = z_{i,0} - z_{i,m+1}x_{m+1} - \cdots - z_{i,m+n}x_{m+n} \quad (i = 1, \ldots, m)$$

Now

$$B = b_1 x_1 + \cdots + b_{m+n}x_{m+n}$$

and substituting for $x_1, \ldots, x_m$ we have

$$B = \sum_{i=1}^{m} b_i(z_{i,0} - z_{i,\,m+1}x_{m+1} - \cdots - z_{i,\,m+n}x_{m+n})$$

$$+ b_{m+1}x_{m+1} + \cdots + b_{m+n}x_{m+n} \qquad (2.2)$$

Comparing constants, and coefficients of $x_{m+1}, \ldots, x_{m+n}$ in Equations (2.1) and (2.2) gives

$$z_{00} = b_0 + b_1 z_{1,0} + \cdots + b_m z_{m0}$$

(which is obvious) and

$$z_{0,m+1} = b_1 z_{1,m+1} + \cdots + b_m z_{m,m+1} - b_{m+1}$$

$$\vdots \qquad \qquad \qquad \qquad \vdots$$

$$z_{0,m+j} = b_1 z_{1,m+j} + \cdots + b_m z_{m,m+j} - b_{m+j}$$

$$\vdots \qquad \qquad \qquad \qquad \vdots$$

$$z_{0,m+n} = b_1 z_{1,m+n} + \cdots + b_m z_{m,m+n} - b_{m+n}$$

We can put this to use in the following way.

Write the coefficients b_i next to x_i on the left of the basic variables, and b_{m+j} above x_{m+j}, the non-basic variables, as we have done already, in brackets. Then, in any column, multiply $z_{i,\,m+j}$ by b_i and add up. Subtracting b_{m+j}, which is at the top of the column, we must obtain the value $z_{0,m+j}$. This provides some check on the calculations, and can also be used when we start with basic variables which appear in the expression of B.

More detail of the Simplex Method follows.

(a) Multiple solutions

We have mentioned that the Simplex Method exhibits only basic solutions. However, an optimal basic feasible solution may not be the only one. For instance, if we change the objective function in Example 1.1 from $4x_1 + 5x_2$ to $4x_1 + x_2$, without changing the constraints, then tableau T_3 changes to that shown in Example 2.1.

Example 2.1

		x_5	x_4	
	B	-1	1	49
(4)	x_1	$-3/7$	$2/7$	6
(1)	x_2	$5/7$	$-1/7$	25
	x_3	1^*	-1	7

and the next tableau is

		x_3	x_4	
	B	1	0	56
(4)	x_1	$3/7$	$-1/7$	9
(1)	x_2	$-5/7$	$4/7^*$	20
	x_5	1	-1	7

This is the tableau of an optimal solution, because there are no negative values in the first, the B-row, but there is a zero entry there. This row means $B + x_3 = 56$. It is clear that the value of B does not change if we increase x_4. The only positive value in the column of x_4 is in the row of x_2, and so we exchange x_2 (making it non-basic) and x_4 (making it basic). After transformation of the tableau, we have then

$$(1)$$

		x_3	x_2	
	B	1	0	56
(4)	x_1	1/4	1/4	14
	x_4	−5/4	7/4	35
	x_5	−1/4	7/4	42

The B-row is unchanged, as a result of the 0 in the B-row of the previous tableau.

We had an optimal basic feasible solution $x' = (9, 20, 0, 0, 7)$ and we have now another, namely $x'' = (14, 0, 0, 35, 42)$. Any weighted average $\lambda_1 x' + \lambda_2 x''$, with $\lambda_1 \geqslant 0$, $\lambda_2 \geqslant 0$, $\lambda_1 + \lambda_2 = 1$ will also be an optimal feasible solution, but it will not be a basic one. Fig. 1.1 makes the result understandable. The pencil of lines $4x_1 + x_2 = $ constant (indicated by broken lines) contain now the line $x_3 = 0$, i.e. $4x_1 + x_2 = 56$. If we consider that line of the pencil as far away from the origin as possible, without leaving the feasible region altogether, then we move to the line $x_3 = 0$. There are two vertices on this line, x' and x'', and each point between these two vertices is clearly also optimal.

If there is more than one 0 in the B-row, then there will be more than two optimal vertices in more than two dimensions. To be sure that one finds every one, systematic methods equivalent to those for finding the way to all points in a maze may be used.

(b) First solution

In Example 1.1 we could easily find a first basic feasible solution by using the slack variables. This was so because the right hand sides of the constraints were positive, and the left hand sides were required to be not larger than those constants.

In Example 1.2 the slack variables could not form the first feasible solution, because the inequalities were in opposite directions. It will also be impossible, in any case, to find a first feasible solution, if no solution exists, because the constraints are contradictory. This latter fact may not be obvious on inspection.

If there is no obvious first solution, then we must use some other method to start our computations.

The method which we now explain adds an 'artificial variable' z_j to the left hand side of the jth constraint, with a positive sign if the constant on the right is positive, and with a negative sign in the opposite case. No artificial variable will be added, however, if a slack variable serves its purpose.

We add to the objective function $-M \Sigma_j z_j$ if we wish to maximize, or $M \Sigma_j z_j$ if we wish to minimize. M is considered to be large, i.e. larger than any number with which it is being compared during computations. This has the effect that when a feasible solution exists, the optimal solution will be found when all z_j are zero. Thus, although we start off with a problem that differs from that we are really concerned with, we shall eventually solve the latter.

Having added the required artificial variables, we can then use as a first basic feasible solution $z_j = c_j$ where the artificial variables are required, while using the slack variables in the other constraints, where appropriate. All other x_j will be set equal to zero. When, at a later stage, one of the artificial variables becomes non-basic, then we exclude it from further consideration — it has served its purpose.

We exhibit this method by using Example 1.2 writing it as minimize

$$20y_1 + 10y_2 + M(z_1 + z_2 + z_3)$$

subject to

$$3y_1 + y_2 - y_3 + z_1 = 3$$
$$4y_1 + 3y_2 - y_4 + z_2 = 6$$
$$y_1 + 2y_2 - y_5 + z_3 = 2$$
$$y_i \geqslant 0, z_j \geqslant 0, \text{ all } i \text{ and } j$$

The first tableau is then

	y_1	y_2	y_3	y_4	y_5	
C	$-20 + 8M$	$-10 + 6M$	$-M$	$-M$	$-M$	$11M$
z_1	3^*	-1	-1	0	0	3
z_2	4	3	0	-1	0	6
z_3	1	2	0	0	1	2

Notice that the C-row has been constructed by making use of the properties of the 'check' as explained in connection with the Simplex Method (p. 22). For instance, the entry in column y_1 is $3M + 4M + M - 20 = -20 + 8M$.

Continuing with the Simplex Method, and dropping any z_j when it becomes non-basic, and hence its value zero, leads to the following succession of tableaus:

	y_2	y_3	y_4	y_5	
C	$-10/3 + 10M/3$	$-20/3 + 5M/3$	$-M$	$-M$	$20+3M$
y_1	$1/3$	$-1/3$	0	0	1
z_2	$5/3$	$4/3$	-1	0	2
z_3	$5/3^*$	$1/3$	0	-1	1

	y_3	y_4	y_5	
C	$-6+M$	$-M$	$-2+M$	$22+M$
y_1	$-2/5$	0	$1/5$	$4/5$
z_2	1^*	-1	1	1
y_2	$1/5$	0	$-3/5$	$3/5$

	y_4	y_5	
C	-6	4	28
y_1	$-2/5$	$3/5$	$6/5$
y_3	-1	1^*	1
y_2	$1/5$	$-4/5$	$2/5$

and, finally

	y_4	y_3	
C	-2	-4	24
y_1	$1/5$	$-3/5$	$3/5$
y_5	-1	1	1
y_2	$-3/5$	$4/5$	$6/5$

If a problem has no solution, this will become clear by the fact that the objective function of the artificial problem will be optimized, but not all z_j will have become zero as yet. This is illustrated in Example 2.2.

Example 2.2
Minimize

$$x_1 + x_2$$

subject to

$$3x_1 - x_2 \leqslant -3$$
$$-4x_1 + 3x_2 \leqslant -6$$
$$x_1, x_2 \geqslant 0$$

It may not be immediately obvious that these constraints are contradictory, but we can see this from Fig. 2.1. The first constraint is equivalent to $9x_1 \leqslant 3x_2 - 9$, and the second to $-4x_1 \leqslant -3x_2 - 6$. If we add them, we have $5x_1 \leqslant -15$, which is plainly impossible with non-negative x_1.

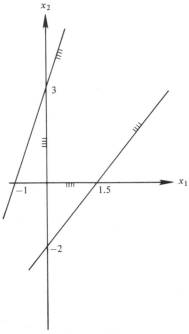

Figure 2.1

In this case we write our problem as minimize

$$x_1 + x_2 + M(z_1 + z_2)$$

subject to

$$3x_1 - x_2 + x_3 - z_1 = -3$$
$$-4x_1 + 3x_2 + x_4 - z_2 = -6$$

and our calculations are as follows:

	x_1	x_2	x_3	x_4	
C	$-1 + M$	$-1 - 2M$	$-M$	$-M$	$9M$
z_1	-3	1	-1	0	3
z_2	$4*$	-3	0	-1	6

	x_2	x_3	x_4	
C	$-7/4 - 5M/4$	$-M$	$-1/4 - 3M/4$	$3/2 + 15M/2$
z_1	$-5/4$	-1	$-3/4$	$15/2$
x_1	$-3/4$	0	$-1/4$	$3/2$

This is an optimal (minimal) solution; all the entries in the C-row are negative, but z_1, an artificial variable, is still basic, which shows that the problem has no solution.

(c) Infinite solutions

It is easily seen that the feasible region need not be bounded on all sides, and the direction to be taken for optimizing may be such that it does not come up against a boundary. This is illustrated in Example 2.3.

Example 2.3
Maximize

$$5x_1 + x_2$$

subject to

$$3x_1 - 2x_2 \leqslant 6$$
$$-4x_1 + 2x_2 \leqslant 4$$
$$x_1, x_2 \geqslant 0$$

see Fig. 2.2.

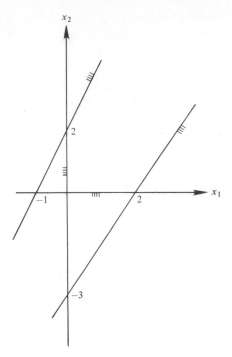

Figure 2.2

We have the tableaus

	x_1	x_2			x_3	x_2	
B	-5	-1	0	B	5/3	$-13/3$	10
x_3	3^*	-2	6	x_1	1/3	$-2/3$	2
x_4	-4	2	4	x_4	4/3	$-2/3$	12

We would now want to make x_2 basic, but there is no positive value in its column to serve as a pivot, and we cannot continue. In fact, we can see algebraically that this means that x_2 can be increased without bounds. The two constraint lines in the last tableau mean

$$x_1 + x_3/3 - 2x_2/3 = 2$$
$$x_4 + 4x_3/3 - 2x_2/3 = 12$$

and we see that any increase in x_2 can be balanced by appropriate increases of x_1 and x_4. Consequently there is no upper limit to $5x_1 + x_2$ either. In such a case we speak of an 'infinite solution'.

(d) Degeneracy

We have seen in Example 2.3 that a basic variable may have the value zero. Such a solution of the constraints is called degenerate. We assume now that given these constraints, we want to maximize $x_1 - x_2$. If we solve the example by the Simplex Method, we start with

	x_1	x_2	
B	-1	1	0
x_3	2	-1	4
x_4	1	-2	2
x_5	1	1	5

We look for the smallest of $4/2, 2/1, 5/1$, and find that the first two ratios are equal. We can therefore take either x_3 or x_4 to be basic and obtain either

	A			or		B		
	x_3	x_2				x_4	x_2	
B	$\frac{1}{2}$	$\frac{1}{2}$	2		B	1	-1	2
x_1	$\frac{1}{2}$	$-\frac{1}{2}$	2		x_3	-2	3	0
x_4	$-\frac{1}{2}$	$-3/2$	0		x_1	1	-2	2
x_5	$-\frac{1}{2}$	$3/2$	3		x_5	-1	3	3

In either case one of the basic variables is zero. This is a consequence of the fact that those two ratios were equal, and of Rule 4 of the Simplex Method.

Of course, both tableaus mean the same point. It may be called $x_2 = x_3 = 0$, or $x_2 = x_4 = 0$, or also $x_3 = x_4 = 0$, but the two tableaus have different functions. The first, A, shows that we have found the optimal basis. The second, B, does not show this. It would, rather, tell us to make x_2 basic, exchanging it for x_3. A further iteration then gives

C

	x_4	x_3	
B	1/3	1/3	2
x_2	−2/3	1/3	0
x_1	−1/3	2/3	2
x_5	1	−1	3

and this is again the same point. This time we see that we have reached, with it, the optimal basis. The optimal point is, in all cases, $(2, 0, 0, 0, 3)$.

We notice, also, that we could have moved from A to C in one step, if we had accepted the value $-3/2$ in row x_4 and column x_2 as a pivot. This would have been against the rules of the Simplex Method but would be allowed because $x_4 = 0$, as we shall see later when we deal with the *Dual Simplex Method*.

We must make a few remarks about a degenerate case. It is possible that the Simplex Method reaches the optimal solution without indicating this in the tableau, as we have seen in tableau B. We had no indication that to choose the exchange (x_1, x_3) might be preferable to the exchange (x_1, x_4).

We also notice that when we moved from B to C, the value of the objective function, namely 2, remained unchanged. This is again a consequence of rule 5, and of the value of the variable to be made non-basic being already zero.

If no basic variable is zero, then the transformation

$$B \rightarrow B - (z_{0,j}z_{i,0})/p > B,$$

because the pivot p as well as the value $z_{i,0}$ of x_i (to be made non-basic) is positive and $z_{0,j}$ is negative; if this were not so, we would not have chosen x_j to be made basic, but if $z_{i,0} = 0$, then B does not change its value.

We have seen that a degenerate point may have different names, and this leads to the possibility that the Simplex Method might run into a loop, producing the same basis over and over again. This might occur when the optimal point has in fact already been reached, but also at an earlier stage. There are indeed cases known when this has happened.

However, there exists a way of avoiding loops in the succession of tableaus. To describe it, we introduce the concept of a 'complete' tableau. The tableaus which we have so far used included only columns for non-basic variables. We call them 'restricted' tableaus. The complete tableau contains columns for all variables. Those for non-basic variables are the same as those in the restricted tableau, while those for the basic variables contain zero everywhere except in their own row, where the entry is 1.

Thus the first complete tableau for Example 1.3 reads:

	x_1	x_2	x_3	x_4	x_5	
B	-1	1	0	0	0	0
x_3	2	-1	1	0	0	4
x_4	1^*	-2	0	1	0	2
x_5	1	1	0	0	1	5

When we transform such a tableau we first enter the solitary 1 and the zeros into the column of the new basic variable, and then transform the other columns as before.

In a diagram in two dimensions, equality of the critical ratios for two basic variables means, as we have seen, that more than two lines pass through the same point, and in n dimensions degeneracy occurs when more than n hyperplanes intersect at the same point. This difficulty disappears if we shift the hyperplanes slightly, parallel to themselves, and find the solution for the perturbed problem, without any points with too many hyperplanes through them. We give now analytical precision to this idea [1].

Add polynomials P_i, defined as

$$P_i = \epsilon^i + \sum_j z_{i,j} \epsilon^j$$

to the values $z_{i,0}$ of the basic variables x_i, where the summation over the subscripts j extends over those of all variables, basic or not (we are dealing now with a complete tableau). We treat the objective function in the same way. Here ϵ stands for a small positive number, so that $a\epsilon^r < b\epsilon^s$ when $r > s$, whatever the values of a and b.

In our example we have then, on the right-hand side

$$B \qquad\qquad -\epsilon + \epsilon^2$$
$$x_3 \qquad\quad 4 + 2\epsilon - \epsilon^2 + \epsilon^3$$
$$x_4 \qquad\quad 2 + \epsilon - 2\epsilon^2 \qquad + \epsilon^4$$
$$x_5 \qquad\quad 5 + \epsilon + \epsilon^2 \qquad\qquad + \epsilon^5$$

If now $4/z_{i,1} > 2/z_{i,2}$, then this is still true of $(4 + P_{i,1})/z_{i,1}$ and $(2 + P_{i,2})/z_{i,2}$, and the addition of the polynomials has no effect. But if $4/z_{i,2} = 2/z_{i,2}$, then the comparison of $2\epsilon/z_{i,1}$ and $\epsilon/z_{i,2}$ is decisive. If these two ratios are still equal, then we proceed to higher powers of ϵ. The tie will be broken at some stage, because in the complete tableau there are columns which contain only one positive value, namely 1, and they contain them in different rows.

It is not necessary to write down the polynomials, because proceeding to the coefficient of higher powers means to proceed, in the tableau, to columns of variables with higher subscripts. Of course, the order of these columns must be kept unaltered throughout.

Turning again to our example, and to the x_1 column, we see that $4/2 = 2/1$, a tie. To resolve it, take the columns of the other variables in succession. Take the column of x_2 first, and compare $-1/2$ and $-2/1$. The latter is smaller, so we exchange x_1 for x_4:

	x_1	x_2	x_3	x_4	x_5	
B	0	−1	0	1	0	2
x_3	0	3*	1	−2	0	0
x_1	1	−2	0	1	0	2
x_5	0	3	0	−1	1	3

Now we have no choice; x_3 must be exchanged for x_2, and the final answer is

	x_1	x_2	x_3	x_4	x_5	
B	0	0	1/3	1/3	0	2
x_2	0	1	1/3	−2/3	0	0
x_1	1	0	2/3	−1/3	0	2
x_5	0	0	−1	1	1	3

This is, in fact, the answer in tableau C.

The Inverse Matrix Method
(revised Simplex Method, Simplex Method using multipliers)

We have explained how the Simplex Method works. There exist variants of this method, which may have advantages in certain circumstances, and we now proceed to explain one of them. Consider Example 2.4.

Example 2.4
Maximize

$$3x_1 + 6x_2 + 2x_3$$

subject to

$$3x_1 + 4x_2 + x_3 \leqslant 20$$

$$x_1 + 3x_2 + 2x_3 \leqslant 10$$

$$x_1 \geqslant 0, x_2 \geqslant 0, x_3 \geqslant 0$$

with its complete tableau, and add a column for B.

	B	x_1	x_2	x_3	x_4	x_5	
B	1	-3	-6	-2	0	0	0
x_4	0	3	4	1	1	0	20
x_5	0	1	3*	2	0	1	10

We denote this tableau, considered as a matrix, by M_0. It describes the linear relationship between x_i and B. After transformation, it describes the same relationship, only in a different way. It follows that any row in the new matrix must be a linear combination of the rows of M_0. Algebraically, this means that M_0 is being pre-multiplied by a square matrix.

Let us look at the matrix which emerges if we use the value marked by an asterisk as pivot:

	B	x_1	x_2	x_3	x_4	x_5		
B	1	-1	0	2	0	2	20	
x_4	0	5/3	0	-5/3	1	-4/3	20/3	= matrix M_1
x_2	0	1/3	1	2/3	0	1/3	10/3	

It is easy to find the square matrix which transforms M_0 into M_1 by pre-multiplication. It is that matrix which transforms the sub-matrix of columns B, x_4, x_5, i.e. the identity matrix, into the new sub-matrix of those columns:

$$E_1 = \begin{pmatrix} 1 & 0 & 2 \\ 0 & 1 & -4/3 \\ 0 & 0 & 1/3 \end{pmatrix}$$

Clearly, $E_1 M_0 = M_1$.

If we look at the sub-matrix of M_0 with columns B, x_4, x_2 in that order, we see that

$$E_1 \begin{pmatrix} 1 & 0 & -6 \\ 0 & 1 & 4 \\ 0 & 0 & 3 \end{pmatrix} = \begin{pmatrix} 1 & 0 & 0 \\ 0 & 1 & 0 \\ 0 & 0 & 1 \end{pmatrix}$$

so that E_1 is the inverse of that sub-matrix, which will become the identity matrix after transforming M_0 into M_1. Because we use matrices like E_1 in the method we are describing, we call it the *Inverse Matrix Method*.

In this method, we shall not compute the whole matrix M_1 and its successors. We have exhibited the whole matrix M_1 merely for the sake of the argument.

A matrix like E_1, which contains the columns of the identity matrix except for one single column, is called an *elementary matrix*. We produce the elementary matrix, which we use to transform one tableau (matrix) into the next, by altering an identity matrix in the following manner.

If the pivot is in the ith row, change the ith column only. Write in this column, in the ith position, the reciprocal of the pivot, and in the other positions divide the corresponding values in the pivotal column of the tableau by the pivot, and change the sign. In our example, this produces E_1 above.

Having produced the appropriate elementary matrix, we must recognize whether the new matrix is optimal, and, if not, we must know its pivotal column. In any case, we shall want to know the values of B and of the basic variables, i.e. the entries in the last column.

To find out if the new matrix is optimal, we must inspect its B-row, and so we pre-multiply the columns of M_0 by the first row of

E_1, and obtain, in our example

$$(1 \quad 0 \quad 2)\begin{pmatrix}1\\0\\0\end{pmatrix} = 1, \quad (1 \quad 0 \quad 2)\begin{pmatrix}-3\\3\\1\end{pmatrix} = -1$$

and so on, i.e. the row

$$1 \quad -1 \quad 0 \quad 2 \quad 0 \quad 2 \quad 20$$

The next pivotal column will therefore be that of x_1, and we need the whole column. We obtain it by pre-multiplying that column of M_0 by E_1

$$\begin{pmatrix}1 & 0 & 2\\0 & 1 & -4/3\\0 & 0 & 1/3\end{pmatrix}\begin{pmatrix}-3\\3\\1\end{pmatrix} = \begin{pmatrix}-1\\5/3\\1/3\end{pmatrix}$$

The last column is

$$\begin{pmatrix}1 & 0 & 2\\0 & 1 & -4/3\\0 & 0 & 1/3\end{pmatrix}\begin{pmatrix}0\\20\\10\end{pmatrix} = \begin{pmatrix}0\\20/3\\10/3\end{pmatrix}$$

We choose the new non-basic variable, to be exchanged for x_1, by finding the smallest of $(20/3)/(5/3)$ and $(10/3)/(1/3)$. It is the first of these, so we exchange x_1 for x_4, and the pivot is $5/3$. The basic variables are then x_1 and x_2.

Compute the next elementary matrix

$$E_2 = \begin{pmatrix}1 & 3/5 & 0\\0 & 3/5 & 0\\0 & -1/5 & 1\end{pmatrix}$$

To ascertain whether the next matrix (tableau), M_2, is optimal, we pre-multiply all columns of M_1 by the first row of E_2; but we have not got all the columns of M_1!

This difficulty is overcome by noticing that M_2 will be equal to $M_2 = E_2M_1 = E_2E_1M_0$. It is therefore sufficient to compute E_2E_1 (which is much simpler to work out than E_2M_1) and then to go back to the original matrix M_0.

Let us then compute $E_2E_1 = E_{2,1}$, say

$$\begin{pmatrix}1 & 3/5 & 0\\0 & 3/5 & 0\\0 & -1/5 & 1\end{pmatrix}\begin{pmatrix}1 & 0 & 2\\0 & 1 & -4/3\\0 & 0 & 1/3\end{pmatrix} = \begin{pmatrix}1 & 3/5 & 6/5\\0 & 3/5 & -4/5\\0 & -1/5 & 3/5\end{pmatrix}$$

The last matrix is, of course, the inverse of the sub-matrix of M_0 consisting of columns of the variables B, x_1 and x_2, namely of

$$\begin{pmatrix} 1 & -3 & -6 \\ 0 & 3 & 4 \\ 0 & 1 & 3 \end{pmatrix}$$

The B-row of M_2 is now computed by pre-multiplying M_0 by the first row of $E_{2,1}$. We obtain

$$1 \quad 0 \quad 0 \quad 1 \quad 3/5 \quad 6/5 \quad 24$$

M_2 is therefore the tableau of the optimal solution, since none of these values is negative. We do not need to compute any pivotal column, but we want to know the values of B, x_1 and x_2, and so we multiply the last column of M_0, i.e.

$$\begin{pmatrix} 0 \\ 20 \\ 10 \end{pmatrix} \quad \text{by } E_{2,1}, \text{ to give} \quad \begin{pmatrix} 24 \\ 4 \\ 2 \end{pmatrix}$$

Finally, we mention some advantages of the Inverse Matrix Method as compared with the original Simplex Method:

(a) Reference to M_0 at each iteration reduces propagation of errors, and reduces the number of multiplications if M_0 is sparse.

(b) The storage requirements for the elementary matrices and their products is $(m + 1)(m + 1)$, to be compared with that for a (restricted) tableau, which is $(n + 1)(m + 1)$. Since usually n is larger than m, there appears to be a saving in the use of the inverse matrix method.

Decomposition algorithm

The algorithm which we shall now describe is useful when dealing with large linear programming problems whose system of constraints can be partitioned into sub-systems, each of which refers to a different set of variables, apart from a few constraints which link all variables together. The objective function will also contain variables from all sub-systems.

Such a pattern appears frequently in large problems, which are so large precisely because they contain conditions for a number of semi-independent organizations (branches in different countries, or manufacturing different products) which are kept together by a central administration. Decentralized planning is then mirrored in the various sub-systems.

If there were no constraints which concerned variables from more than one sub-system, then we could split the objective function appropriately and optimize each portion, subject to its own constraints. If there are linking constraints, then we could ignore them to begin with, and see if the optimal values obtained for the sub-system satisfy the linking constraints as well. If they do, then the optimal solution for the overall problem has been found. Otherwise we must make adjustments. We imagine that the central authority — which knows that the values presented to it from the sub-systems do not satisfy all constraints — issues orders to the several sub-authorities about how to adjust their results.

We illustrate the algorithm by considering the problem of Example 2.5.

Example 2.5
Maximize

$$3x_1 + 6x_2 + 2x_3$$

subject to

$$3x_1 + 4x_2 + x_3 \leqslant 20$$
$$x_1 + 3x_2 + 2x_3 \leqslant 10$$
$$x_1 - x_2 \qquad \leqslant 3$$
$$x_1 + x_2 \qquad \leqslant 6$$
$$x_3 \leqslant 2$$
$$x_1, x_2, x_3 \geqslant 0$$

This is the same as Example 2.4, with the addition of the two sub-systems

$$x_1 - x_2 \leqslant 3$$
$$x_1 + x_2 \leqslant 6$$ and $$x_3 \leqslant 2$$

Any set of variables which satisfy all constraints must, of course, satisfy those of the subproblems in particular, and to begin with, we deal with the latter. They are illustrated in Fig. 2.3(a) and (b).

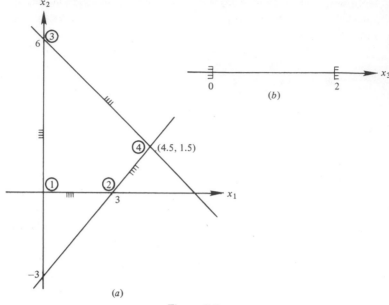

Figure 2.3

The feasible region in Fig. 2.3(a) has four vertices, namely

$$(x_{1,1}, x_{2,1}) = (0, 0), \quad (x_{1,2}, x_{2,2}) = (3, 0)$$

$$(x_{1,3}, x_{2,3}) = (0, 6), \quad (x_{1,4}, x_{2,4}) = (4.5, 1.5)$$

and that in Fig. 2.3(b) has the two vertices $x_{3,1} = 0$, and $x_{3,2} = 2$.

Each point of a feasible region, which is not unbounded, can be considered to be the centre of gravity, when appropriate weights are attached to the vertices (Theorem 1.3). Algebraically, this means that any feasible point in Fig. 2.3(a) has co-ordinates

$$x_1 = 0.\lambda_1 + 3\lambda_2 + 0.\lambda_3 + 4.5\lambda_4$$

$$x_2 = 0.\lambda_1 + 0.\lambda_2 + 6\lambda_3 + 1.5\lambda_4$$

with $\lambda_1 + \lambda_2 + \lambda_3 + \lambda_4 = 1$, all $\lambda_i \geqslant 0$

and those in Fig. 2.3(b) have co-ordinates

$$x_3 = 0.\mu_1 + 2\mu_2$$

with $\mu_1 + \mu_2 = 1, \mu_1, \mu_2 \geqslant 0$.

We introduce these expressions for x_1, x_2 and x_3 into the first two constraints, which contain all variables, and also into the objective function. With slack variables x_4 and x_5, our problem is then maximize

$$9\lambda_2 + 36\lambda_3 + 22.5\lambda_4 + 4\mu_2$$

subject to

$$9\lambda_2 + 24\lambda_3 + 19.5\lambda_4 + 2\mu_2 + x_4 = 20$$

$$3\lambda_2 + 18\lambda_3 + 9\lambda_4 + 4\mu_2 + x_5 = 10$$

$$\lambda_1 + \lambda_2 + \lambda_3 + \lambda_4 = 1$$

$$\mu_1 + \mu_2 = 1$$

$$\lambda_1, \lambda_2, \lambda_3, \lambda_4, \mu_1, \mu_2, x_4, x_5 \geqslant 0$$

This problem is called the *master problem*, the sets of the λ and of the μ are referred to as *proposals*, and the last two constraints are *convexity constraints*.

We were able to write the master problem in this form because we knew the vertices of the feasible regions of the sub-problems. However, to find all vertices of a convex region, although possible, might involve excessive computations, and it is fortunately not necessary, as we shall see.

We note here that in the first constraint λ_i is multiplied by $3x_{1,i} + 4x_{2,i}$, in the second constraint by $x_{1,i} + 3x_{2,i}$, and in the objective function by $3x_{1,i} + 6x_{2,i}$. μ_j is multiplied in the first constraint by $x_{3,j}$ and in the second by $2x_{3,j}$, and in the objective function by $2x_{3,j}$. Because $x_{3,1} = 0$, this reduces to 0 for $j = 1$, and to $2\mu_2$, $4\mu_2$, and $4\mu_2$, in this order.

For a first solution we can use x_4, x_5, λ_1 and μ_1 as basic variables, because the first vertex is $(0, 0)$ in (a), and (0) in (b) (if this were not so, we would have to apply some other method to find a first solution, but this is not germane to the Decomposition Algorithm, and need not detain us here). Our first tableau is then T_0

	B	λ_i	μ_j	x_4	x_5	
B	1	$-3x_{1,i} - 6x_{2,i}$	$-2x_{3,j}$	0	0	0
x_4	0	$3x_{1,i} + 4x_{2,i}$	$x_{3,j}$	1	0	20
x_5	0	$x_{1,i} + 3x_{2,i}$	$2x_{3,j}$	0	1	10
λ_1	0	1	0	0	0	1
μ_1	0	0	1	0	0	1

The next step depends on whether there is a negative value in the B-row. In the present case we see immediately that $-2x_{3,j}$ is negative for $j = 2$ ($-2x_{3,2} = -4$), but such an obvious opportunity does not always present itself, and we shall proceed systematically, dealing first with the λ_i.

We ask, therefore, if $-3x_{1,i} - 6x_{2,i}$ is negative for any value of i. This question can be answered by asking for the minimum of $-3x_1 - 6x_2$, subject to $x_1 - x_2 \leqslant 3$, $x_1 + x_2 \leqslant 6$, x_1, $x_2 \geqslant 0$ because we know that the minimum will be obtained in a vertex of the region defined by these inequalities.

Solving this small linear programming problem, we find that the minimum occurs at $(x_1, x_2) = (0, 6)$, vertex 3 in Fig. 2.3(a). The λ_3 column is

$$
\begin{array}{lcc}
-36 & & 0 \\
24 & & 20 \\
18^* & \text{and comparing it with} & 10 \\
1 & & 1 \\
0 & & 1
\end{array}
$$

we find the pivot where indicated. We shall exchange λ_3 for x_5.

In the spirit of the Inverse Matrix Method we construct

$$
E_1 = \begin{pmatrix}
1 & 0 & 2 & 0 & 0 \\
0 & 1 & -4/3 & 0 & 0 \\
0 & 0 & 1/18 & 0 & 0 \\
0 & 0 & -1/18 & 1 & 0 \\
0 & 0 & 0 & 0 & 1
\end{pmatrix}
$$

and pre-multiplying T_0 by the first row of E_1, and the last column of T_0 by E_1, we obtain the new B-row, and the column of constants of the next tableau, T_1.

	B	λ_i	μ_j	x_4	x_5	
B	1	$-x_{1,i}$	$2x_{3,j}$	0	2	20
x_4						20/3
λ_3						5/9
λ_1						4/9
μ_1						1

To continue, we look again at the B-row and the column λ_i. In which vertex of Fig 2.3(a) is $-x_{1,i}$ most negative? We find the answer by inspection: in vertex 4, where $-x_{1,4} = -4.5$. The λ_4 column was originally

(B)	-22.5
(x_4)	19.5
(x_5)	9
(λ_1)	1
(μ_1)	0

and pre-multiplied by E_1, it is now

(B)	-4.5
(x_4)	7.5
(λ_3)	0.5
(λ_1)	0.5^*
(μ_1)	0

Comparing it with

$$\begin{matrix} 20 \\ 20/3 \\ 10/3 \\ 5/9 \\ 4/9 \\ 1 \end{matrix}$$

we have the pivot where indicated. We shall exchange λ_4 for λ_1.

We construct

$$E_2 = \begin{pmatrix} 1 & 0 & 0 & 9 & 0 \\ 0 & 1 & 0 & -15 & 0 \\ 0 & 0 & 1 & -1 & 0 \\ 0 & 0 & 0 & 2 & 0 \\ 0 & 0 & 0 & 0 & 1 \end{pmatrix}$$

and

$$E_{2,1} = E_2 \cdot E_1 = \begin{pmatrix} 1 & 0 & 3/2 & 9 & 0 \\ 0 & 1 & -1/2 & -15 & 0 \\ 0 & 0 & 1/9 & -1 & 0 \\ 0 & 0 & -1/9 & 2 & 0 \\ 0 & 0 & 0 & 0 & 1 \end{pmatrix}$$

Pre-multiplying T_1 by the first row of $E_{2,1}$, and the last column of T_0 by $E_{2,1}$ (or, alternatively, the last column of T_1 by E_2) we obtain the B-row and the column of constants of the next tableau, T_2.

	B	λ_i	μ_j	x_4	x_5	
B	1	$(-3x_{1,i}/2 - 3x_{2,i}/2 + 9)$	$x_{3,j}$	0	3/2	24
x_4						0
λ_3						1/9
λ_4						8/9
μ_1						1

To continue, we look again for the minimum of

$$-3x_1/2 - 3x_2/2 + 9$$

subject to

$$x_1 - x_2 \leqslant 3, x_1 + x_2 \leqslant 6, x_1, x_2 \geqslant 0$$

The result is 0. None of the feasible values of the objective function is negative. We must still look at the μ_j column. However, no $x_{3,j}$ ($j = 1, 2$) is negative, and there is no negative value in the B-row for x_4 or x_5 either. Hence T_2 is the final tableau, giving us all the necessary information. We want, of course, the values of x_i, not those of λ_i and μ_j. Now

$$x_1 = 0.\lambda_1 + 3\lambda_2 + 0.\lambda_3 + 4.5\lambda_4 = 4.5 \times 8/9 = 4$$

$$x_2 = 0.\lambda_1 + 0.\lambda_2 + 6\lambda_3 + 1.5\lambda_4 = 6 \times 1/9 + 1.5 \times 8/9 = 2$$

With $B = 24$, this is the final answer.

Parametric programming

We have assumed, until now, that the values of the constants in our formulations are precisely known, but situations do arise where this is not so, and where we can only place such values with confidence within certain intervals. It is then relevant to ask whether, and how, the precise places of the values within their intervals affect the final answer. We deal here with a few simple cases which fall within this area of problems.

We shall deal first with a case where coefficients of the objective function depend on a parameter, then with a case where the r.h.s. of a constraint depends on a parameter, and finally with a case where a coefficient in one of the constraints is a parameter. These examples will demonstrate the fundamental idea of the procedure.

We take again our Example 1.1, but we assume now that the objective function to be maximized is

$$B = (4 - t)x_1 + (5 - t)x_2$$

while the constraints are again

$$4x_1 + x_2 \leqslant 56$$
$$5x_1 + 3x_2 \leqslant 105$$
$$x_1 + 2x_2 < 56$$

We start with some value of the parameter $t = t_0$, say, and solve for it. We then decide within which interval of t_0 the resulting values of the x_i remain unaltered.

Let us choose $t = 5$. Then the first tableau

	x_1	x_2	
B	$-4 + t$	$-5 + t$	0
x_3	4	1	56
x_4	5	3	105
x_5	1	2	56

is also the final tableau, because then $-4 + t \geqslant 0$ and $-5 + t \geqslant 0$. It will also be the final tableau for all $t \geqslant 5$. The objective function has value 0, and $x_1 = x_2 = 0$ as well.

When $t = 5$, the answer is not unique, though. In this case we have to maximize $-x_1$, i.e. to minimize x_1. Looking at Fig. 1.1 we see that this leads to two vertices, and all the points on the straight line between them. When t changes, then the direction of the lines $(4 - t)x_1 + (5 - t)x_2$ = constant turns, and it is seen that the optimal vertex will also change.

If $t \leqslant 5$, then we can make x_2 basic, exchanging it for x_5, and we have then

	x_1	x_5	
B	$-3/2 + t/2$	$5/2 - t/2$	$140 - 28t$
x_3	$7/2$	$-1/2$	28
x_4	$7/2$	$-3/2$	21
x_2	$1/2$	$1/2$	28

We see that as long as $-3/2 + t/2 \geqslant 0$ and $5/2 - t/2 \geqslant 0$, i.e. when t is between 3 and 5, the objective function has value $140 - 28t$, and $x_1 = 0$, $x_2 = 28$ (another vertex in Fig. 1.1). When t is precisely 3, the answer is again not unique.

Now let $t \leqslant 3$. Then $-3/2 + t/2 \leqslant 0$, and we exchange x_1 for x_4. The next tableau will be

	x_4	x_5	
B	$3/7 - t/7$	$13/7 - 2t/7$	$149 - 31t$
x_3	-1	1	7
x_1	$2/7$	$-3/7$	6
x_2	$-1/7$	$5/7$	25

When $t \leqslant 3$, then $3/7 - t/7$ as well as $13/7 - 2t/7$ are non-negative, so that this remains the final tableau for all values of t less than 3. At precisely 3 we have an alternative solution, as we already know.

When $t = 0$, then $B = 149$, and we have recovered the result of Example 1.1. We note that it is quite possible that one of the intervals of t constructed in this manner reduces to one single point.

Now we turn to cases where parameters appear in constraints. For instance, modify Example 1.1 as follows. Maximize

$$4x_1 + 5x_2$$

subject to

$$4x_1 + x_2 \leqslant 56 + t$$
$$5x_1 + 3x_2 \leqslant 105$$
$$x_1 + 2x_2 \leqslant 56$$
$$x_1, x_2 \geqslant 0$$

With regard to Fig. 1.1, this means that we move the line $x_3 = 0$ parallel to itself in either direction, dependent on whether t is positive or negative. We note also, without any computation, that there is no answer when $t < -56$, since $4x_1 + x_2$ cannot be negative, when x_1 and x_2 are non-negative.

Our first tableau is now

	x_1	x_2	
B	-4	-5	0
x_3	4	1	$56 + t$
x_4	5	3	105
x_5	1	2	56

Let us try to make x_2 basic.

$105/3$ is larger than $56/2$, so x_4 does not qualify to be exchanged for x_2. The choice lies between x_3 and x_5, and the decision depends on comparing $(56 + t)/1$ and $56/2$, i.e. on whether t is smaller or larger than -28.

First, let $-56 \leqslant t \leqslant -28$, then we obtain

	x_1	x_3	
B	16	5	$280 + 5t$
x_2	4	1	$56 + t$
x_4	-7	-3	$-63 - 3t$
x_5	-7	-2	$-56 - 2t$

and this is the final, optimal tableau for those values of t.

When $t \geqslant -28$, we have

	x_1	x_5	
B	$-3/2$	$5/2$	140
x_3	$7/2$	$-1/2$	$28 + t$
x_4	$7/2$	$-3/2$	21
x_2	$1/2$	$1/2$	28

This indicates a basic solution, but not an optimal one for any t. We must exchange x_1, either for x_3 (if $-28 \leqslant t \leqslant -7$) or for x_4 (if $t \geqslant -7$). In these two cases we obtain

	x_3	x_5	
B	$3/7$	$16/7$	$152 + 3t/7$
x_1	$2/7$	$-1/7$	$8 + 2t/7$
x_4	-1	-1	$-7 - t$
x_2	$-1/7$	$4/7$	$24 - t/7$

or

	x_4	x_5	
B	$3/7$	$13/7$	149
x_3	-1	1	$7 + t$
x_1	$2/7$	$-31/7$	6
x_2	$-1/7$	$5/7$	25

With $t = 0$, we have in the latter tableau again the result of Example 1.1.

As our last example, let us take the following. Maximize

$$4x_1 + 5x_2$$

subject to

$$tx_1 + x_2 \leqslant 56$$
$$5x_1 + 3x_2 \leqslant 105$$
$$x_1 + 2x_2 \leqslant 56$$
$$x_1, x_2 \geqslant 0$$

with the first tableau

	x_1	x_2	
B	-4	-5	0
x_3	t	1	56
x_4	5	3	105
x_5	1	2	56

leading to

	x_1	x_5	
B	$-3/2$	$5/2$	140
x_3	$t-\frac{1}{2}$	$-1/2$	28
x_4	$6/2$	$-3/2$	21
x_2	$1/2$	$1/2$	28

This indicates again a vertex (which we already know), but no optimal solution for any value of t.

We must make x_1 basic. The choice of the new non-basic variable, x_3 or x_4, depends on the comparison of $28/(t-\frac{1}{2})$ with $21/(7/2) = 6$. Hence we have

	x_4	x_5	
B	$3/7$	$13/7$	149
x_3	$(1-2t)/7$	$(-5+3t)/7$	$31-6t$
x_1	$2/7$	$-3/7$	6
x_2	$-1/7$	$5/7$	25

when $t \leqslant 31/6$ (when $t = 4$, this brings us back to Example 1.1) and

	x_3	x_5	
B	$3/(2t-1)$	$(5t-4)/(2t-1)$	$(280t-56)/(2t-1)$
x_1	$2/(2t-1)$	$-1/(2t-1)$	$56/(2t-1)$
x_4	$-7/(2t-1)$	$(-3t+5)/(2t-1)$	$(42t-217)/(2t-1)$
x_2	$-1/(2t-1)$	$t/(2t-1)$	$(56t-56)/2t-1$

when $t \geqslant 31/6$. If more than one parameter appears in a problem, the procedure for solving it is more lengthy, but it does not involve any new principle.

Problems

2.1 (a) Maximize $5x_1 + 6x_2$ subject to

$$3x_1 + 4x_2 \leqslant 18$$
$$2x_1 + x_2 \leqslant 7$$
$$x_1, x_2 \geqslant 0$$

(b) Minimize $5x_1 - 6x_2$ subject to

$$3x_1 + 4x_2 \leqslant 18$$
$$2x_1 + x_2 \leqslant 7$$
$$x_1, x_2 \geqslant 0$$

2.2. Maximize $6x_1 + 8x_2$ subject to

$$3x_1 + 4x_2 \leqslant 18$$
$$2x_1 + x_2 \leqslant 7$$
$$x_1, x_2 \geqslant 0$$

2.3. Minimize $5x_1 - 6x_2$ subject to

$$3x_1 + 4x_2 \leqslant 18$$
$$4x_1 + 2x_2 \leqslant 9$$
$$x_1, x_2 \geqslant 0$$

2.4. Maximize $x_1 + 8x_2 + 5x_3$ subject to

$$x_1 + 4x_2 + 5x_3 \leqslant 7$$
$$3x_1 + 4x_2 \leqslant 18$$
$$2x_1 + x_2 \leqslant 7$$
$$x_1, x_2, x_3 \geqslant 0$$

2.5. Maximize $(5 - t)x_1 + (6 - t)x_2$ subject to

$$3x_1 + 4x_2 \leqslant 18$$
$$2x_1 + x_2 \leqslant 7$$
$$x_1, x_2 \geqslant 0$$

dependent on values of t.

2.6. Maximize $x_1 + x_2$ subject to

$$-x_1 + x_2 \leqslant 1$$
$$x_1 - x_2 \leqslant 1$$
$$x_1, x_2 \geqslant 0$$

2.7. Solve Problem 1.1 by an application of the Simplex algorithm.

2.8. An establishment consists of three grades: g_1, g_2 and g_3. 80% of the personnel in g_1 remain in this grade for another year. 10% are promoted into g_2, while 10% leave altogether. Of those in g_2, 60% remain for another year, 20% move into g_3 and 20% leave. Of those in grade g_3 80% stay on and 20% leave.

New members are recruited into g_1 and g_2 but none into g_3.

Which are the proportionate numbers in the various grades which can be maintained for another year, with appropriate recruitment?

CHAPTER 3

Duality

As a counterpart, or obverse, of a problem:

$$\text{maximize} \quad b'x, \text{ subject to } Ax \leqslant c, x \geqslant 0 \tag{P}$$

consider its 'dual':

$$\text{minimize} \quad c'y, \text{ subject to } A'y \geqslant b, y \geqslant 0 \tag{D}$$

The original, 'primal' problem, has m inequality constraints, in n variables, while the 'dual' problem has n inequality constraints and m variables. Also, in the problem to be maximized the left hand side must not exceed the right hand side, while in that to be minimized, the left hand side is not smaller than the right hand side. In either problem, though, the variables are restricted to having non-negative values.

For instance, the dual to Example 1.1 is, minimize

$$56y_3 + 105y_4 + 56y_5$$

subject to

$$4y_3 + 5y_4 + \ y_5 \geqslant 4$$
$$y_3 + 3y_4 + 2y_5 \geqslant 5$$
$$y_3, y_4, y_5 \geqslant 0$$

It is, of course, immaterial which subscripts we choose for the variables, and for reasons which will emerge, it is convenient to start with subscripts of y after we have used the subscripts of x.

To have another example, consider the two problems, dual to one another

Example 3.1

Maximize   Minimize

$$3x_1 + 6x_2 + 2x_3 = B \qquad\qquad 20y_4 + 10y_5 = C$$

subject to   subject to

$$3x_1 + 4x_2 + x_3 \leqslant 20$$ $$3y_4 + y_5 \geqslant 3$$

$$x_1 + 3x_2 + 2x_3 \leqslant 10$$ $$4y_4 + 3y_5 \geqslant 6$$

$$y_4 + 2y_5 \geqslant 2$$

$$x_1, x_2, x_3 \geqslant 0$$ $$y_4, y_5 \geqslant 0$$

(this is Example 2.4)   (this is Example 1.2, with a change
                                        of notation)

If we introduce slack variables, we call them, respectively, x_4, x_5 and y_1, y_2, y_3, so that the slack variables in one of the systems have the subscripts of the original variables in the other.

A first solution of the maximizing problem is easily seen, by inspection, to be $x_4 = 20, x_5 = 10$, choosing the slack variables to be basic. In the minimizing problem $y_1 = -3, y_2 = -6$, and $y_3 = -2$ are not feasible. We could solve this problem by the M-method, as we have done earlier; however, we might try and see what happens if we insist on using the slack variables as basic ones to begin with. In restricted tableau form we have then in the two cases, as first tableaus

	x_1	x_2	x_3			y_4	y_5	
B	-3	-6	-2	0	C	-20	-10	0
x_4	3	4	1	20	y_1	-3	-1	-3
x_5	1	3*	2	10	y_2	-4	-3*	-6
					y_3	-1	-2	-2

The x tableau exhibits a feasible basic solution, as all Simplex tableaus do. The B-row contains negative entries, and these indicate that the maximum has not been found as yet. The y-tableau, on the other hand, gives inadmissible values to the variables y_1, y_2 and y_3, but the C-row has just the right signs for minimizing. We call a tableau with this property 'dual feasible'.

We call the relationship between the two tableaus *duality*. The rows in one of them correspond to the columns in the other, with changed signs, except that the signs in the B-row are the same as those in the column of constants of the minimizing problem (but the signs in the C-row are not those of the column of constants in the maximizing problem!). In particular, the present value of B equals the present value of C. Moreover, the labels of the rows in one tableau have the same subscripts as the labels of the columns in the other.

Let us now transform the x-tableau by exchanging x_2 and x_5, according to the Simplex rules (the pivot is indicated by an asterisk), and write down the dual of the emerging tableau:

	x_1	x_5	x_3			y_4	y_2	
B	-1	2	2	20	C	$-20/3$	$-10/3$	20
x_4	$5/3*$	$-4/3$	$-5/3$	20/3	y_1	$-5/3*$	$-1/3$	-1
x_2	$1/3$	$1/3$	$2/3$	10/3	y_5	$4/3$	$-1/3$	2
					y_3	$5/3$	$-2/3$	2

The resulting y-tableau is also a transformation of the first y-tableau according to the Simplex rules, if we choose the pivot (-3) corresponding to that of the first x-tableau, namely, 3. Since the rules of the Simplex Method are simply the algebraic rules of substitution, the lines of the new y-tableau are again legitimate transformations of the constraints of the minimizing problem. The derivation of the second tableau can be described, without reference to the x-tableau, as follows:

(a) Choose the row of a variable with negative value.

(b) In this row choose a pivot in that column in which $|\, z_{j,0}/z_{i,j}\,|$ is smallest, but taking only negative $z_{i,j}$ into account. In this notation i is the row of the variable chosen, and $z_{j,0}$ is the value in the C-row, in column j. If

$$\min |\, z_{j,0}/z_{i,j}\,| = |\, z_{j_0,0}/z_{i,j_0}\,|$$

then z_{i,j_0} is the pivot (we have used the modulus sign $|.|$ because the method is equally applicable to maximizing problems, where $z_{j,0}$ would be positive in a dual feasible tableau, while $z_{i,j}$ would still have to be negative.

(c) Apply the rules of the Simplex transformation.

The method just described is the *Dual Simplex Method*. It is applicable when we start from a dual feasible tableau.

We carry on with our example:

	x_4	x_5	x_3			y_1	y_2	
B	3/5	6/5	1	24	C	−4	−2	24
x_1	3/5	−4/5	−1	4	y_4	−3/5	1/5	3/5
x_2	−1/5	3/5	1	2	y_5	4/5	−3/5	6/5
					y_3	1	−1	1

Now all values in the B-row are positive, the largest feasible value of B has been reached. The dual relationship ensures that all values of the variables in the y-tableau are also positive. We have reached a feasible minimum of C as well.

The answer is, of course, the same as that obtained earlier in Example 1.2, although the subscripts of the variables are different.

It follows from the dual relationship that acceptable signs for the values of the variables as well as for the coefficients of the objective functions are reached at the same stage. We see that:

1. If one of the two dual problems has a finite solution, then so has the other.
2. The two optimal values are equal.

We shall refer to these two statements as the *Duality Theorem*.

For any x which satisfies the constraints of (P), and any y which satisfies those of (D), we have

$$b'x \leqslant x'A'y \leqslant c'y$$

Hence, if we find vectors x^0 and y^0 which satisfy their respective constraints, and such that $b'x^0 = c'y^0$, then x^0 is the solution of (P), and y^0 is the solution of (D). We express this fact in the form of a *sufficiency theorem*. A sufficient condition for x^0 to solve (P) is the existence of a vector y^0 such that $A'y^0 \geqslant b, y^0 \geqslant 0$, and $b'x^0 = c'y^0$.

Conversely, the following *necessity theorem* follows from the Duality Theorem. If a finite vector x^0 solves (P), then there must exist a finite vector y^0 which solves (D), and such that $b'x^0 = c'y^0$.

Now consider the expression

$$(c - Ax^0)'y^0 + (A'y^0 - b)'x^0$$

Since $c'y^0 = b'x^0$ and $(Ax^0)'y^0 = (A'y^0)'x^0$, this expression is zero, but $c - Ax^0$ is the vector of slack variables $\mathbf{x}^0$, and $A'y^0 - b$ is the vector of slack variables y^0. Thus we can write

$$x^{0\prime}y^0 = y^{0\prime}x^0 = 0$$

and since all components of x^0, x^0, y^0, y^0 are non-negative, each term in the two scalar products must vanish.

If we recall the way in which we have applied subscripts to x and y, and that the subscripts of the slack variables of one problem are those of the original variables in the other problem, we find that

$$x_i^0 y_i^0 = x_j^0 y_j^0 = 0$$

for all $i = 1, \ldots, n$, and all $j = 1, \ldots, m$. We call this relationship 'complementary slackness' [12].

We prove a further theorem, concerning an expression called the Lagrangean of the two dual problems. Let us recall from the algebraic theory of optimization with side conditions that if we wish to maximize, or to minimize, a function $f(x)$ subject to $g_1(x) = 0, \ldots, g_m(x) = 0$, then we form the Lagrangean $L(x) = f(x) + \lambda_1 g_1(x) + \cdots + \lambda_m g_m(x)$, and set the derivatives of $L(x)$ with regard to x and to all λ_i equal to zero. The solution of the system leads, under fairly general conditions, which do not concern us here, to the solution of the optimizing problem. Let us formally copy this procedure.

If we have to maximize $b'x$, subject to $c - Ax \geqslant 0$, we introduce the vector y as a vector of Lagrangean multipliers and form the expression

$$b'x + y'(c - Ax) = \Phi(x, y)$$

say. If we start from the dual problem, that of minimizing $c'y$ subject to $b - A'y \leqslant 0$, we introduce the Lagrangean vector x and form

$$c'y + x'(b - A'y) = b'x + y'(c - Ax)$$

again $\Phi(x, y)$. More simply, in either case $\Phi(x, y) = b'x + c'y - x'A'y$ is the Lagrangean of either of two dual problems.

Now introduce the requirements $x \geqslant 0$ and $y \geqslant 0$. Let x^0 and y^0 be solutions of (P) and (D), respectively, then

$$\Phi(x^0, y) - \Phi(x^0, y^0) = b'x^0 + y'(c - Ax^0) - b'x^0 - y^{0\prime}(c - Ax^0)$$
$$= y'(c - Ax^0) - y^{0\prime}(c - Ax^0)$$

The first term is non-negative, the second is zero by complementary slackness. Hence

$$\Phi(x^0, y) - \Phi(x^0, y^0) \geqslant 0 \qquad (3.1)$$

Also

$$\Phi(x^0, y^0) - \Phi(x, y^0) = c'y^0 + x^{0\prime}(b - A'y^0) - c'y^0$$
$$- x'(b - A'y^0) = x^{0\prime}(b - A'y^0) - x'(b - A'y^0)$$

The first term is zero by complementary slackness, the second is non-negative. Hence

$$\Phi(x^0, y^0) - \Phi(x, y^0) \geqslant 0 \qquad (3.2)$$

Combining Equations (3.1) and (3.2), we have

$$\Phi(x^0, y) \geqslant \Phi(x^0, y^0) \geqslant \Phi(x, y^0)$$

By an obvious geometric analogy, we call (x^0, y^0) a saddle point of the surface $\Phi(x, y)$ (x and y are vectors).

We shall now deal with some special aspects of duality theory.

We know that if the B-row of a tableau contains a zero value, then this points to the existence of an alternative solution. The dual to this situation is a degenerate solution with a zero basic variable. If we have a dual feasible tableau, and the row with the zero variable contains a negative entry, then we can continue with the Dual Simplex Method to an alternative dual feasible solution.

If we had done this in Example 1.3, tableau A, we would have obtained at once tableau C. The alternative tableau B in that example is not dual feasible.

Now suppose the primal problem has an infinite solution. This means, in tableau terms, that there is a column whose variable might be made basic, but there is no positive entry in that column which could serve as the pivot. Suppose this happens in a maximizing problem, and that the column is

x_j

$b_j \quad (< 0)$

$z_{1,j} \quad (\leqslant 0)$

.

.

$z_{m,j} \quad (\leqslant 0),$

then the corresponding row in the dual problem reads

$$y_j - z_{1,j}y_1 - \cdots - z_{m,j}y_m = b_j$$

However, this is impossible, because the right hand side is negative, and the left hand side must be non-negative. The same argument applies, with the necessary changes, when we start from a minimizing problem. We have shown that if a problem has no finite optimal solution, then its dual problem has contradictory constraints.

The converse of this theorem does not hold. It is quite possible that a problem has contradictory constraints, and its dual has no unbounded optimal solution either. It cannot have a finite solution, of course, as a consequence of the duality theorem, and in such a case it would also have contradictory constraints. The following example shows a pair of dual problems, each with contradictory constraints.

Example 3.2

Minimize $2x_1 - x_2$ Minimize $y_3 - 2y_4$

subject to   subject to

$$x_1 - x_2 \leqslant 1$$ $$y_3 - y_4 \geqslant 2$$

$$x_1 + x_2 \leqslant -2$$ $$-y_3 + y_4 \geqslant -1$$

$$x_1, x_2 \geqslant 0$$ $$y_3, y_4 \geqslant 0$$

The constraints of either problem are contradictory. They amount to $a - b \leqslant 1, a - b \geqslant 2$.

If in a linear programming problem $x_i \geqslant 0$ is not specifically required, then we can replace x_i by $x_i^{(\prime)} - x_i^{(\prime\prime)}, x_i^{(\prime)}, x_i^{(\prime\prime)} \geqslant 0$. When none of the variables is required to be non-negative, and we have the problem to maximize

$$b'x, \text{ i.e. } b'x^{(\prime)} - b'x^{(\prime\prime)}$$

subject to

$$Ax \leqslant c, \text{ i.e. } Ax^{(\prime)} - Ax^{(\prime\prime)} \leqslant c$$

(but not $x \geqslant 0$ as well) then its dual will be minimize $c'y$ subject to

$$A'y \geqslant b, -A'y \geqslant -b, y \geqslant 0$$

which is the same as subject to

$$A'y = b, y \geqslant 0$$

In other words, the constraints which correspond to variables which may have any sign are equations.

In the same way we can show that the dual to minimize $c'x$ subject to

$$Ax \geqslant b \quad \text{(but not } x \geqslant 0 \text{ necessarily)}$$

is maximize $b'y$ subject to

$$A'y = c, y \geqslant 0$$

Conversely, if the constraints of a problem are equations, then the variables of its dual are not restricted to be non-negative.

We now turn to uses which can be made of the concept of duality, and of its features.

(a) Shadow costs

Look again at the final tableau of Example 1.1 and of its dual.

			x_5	x_4		
		B	13/7	3/7		149
(4)		x_1	−3/7	2/7		6
(5)		x_2	5/7	−1/7		25
		x_3	1	−1		7
			y_1	y_2	(56) y_3	
		C	−6	−25	−7	149
(56)		y_5	3/7	−5/7	−1	13/7
(105)		y_4	−2/7	1/7	1	3/7

The final value of B, 149, equals $4 \times 6 + 5 \times 25$. It also equals (see the y-tableau) $56 \times 13/7 + 105 \times 3/7$. The values 56, 105, 56 were the right hand sides in Example 1.1 (and hence the coefficients of the objective function of its dual). Suppose now that 57 rather than 56 were available of raw material R_3, to which the variable x_5 refers:

this would increase the right hand side of the first constraint from 56 to 57, and the final value of B as well as of C by $(57 - 56) \times 13/7$. Similarly, if the right hand side of the constraint to which x_4 refers were increased by 1, from 105 to 106, the value of B would be increased by $3/7$.

On the other hand, if the availability of raw material R_1 were increased, this would not make any difference to the final result. This is understandable, because R_1 is not completely used up in the optimal plan: the slack variable x_3 is positive.

We can now ask the following question: how much are we prepared to pay for an increase of a raw material? The answer follows from our analysis above: we are not prepared to pay anything for more of R_1, however, we are prepared to pay up to $13/7$ for one unit of R_3, and up to $3/7$ for one unit of R_2. (Of course, we shall not be willing to acquire unlimited amounts at these prices; we come back to this point later.) We have come to this conclusion by looking at the right-hand side of the dual tableau. But it is not necessary for this purpose to write down that dual tableau, because the relevant values are already exhibited in the primal tableau, in the B-row.

In view of this interpretation of the values in the B-row of the final tableau, we call them *shadow prices*, or *shadow costs*. An analysis of the effects of changes in the constants of a problem is referred to as *sensitivity analysis*. Parametric programming, which we have discussed above, belongs also into this field.

The argument above was based on the final tableau, which indicates the best plan. Thus it is only valid as long as the tableau remains optimal, after the changes in availabilities of the raw materials. We ask therefore, how far we can go increasing availabilities, i.e. how much may we buy at the shadow prices.

Assume, then that we increase the availability of R_3 by Δ. If the tableau remains optimal, then the profit is increased by $13\Delta/7$. But is either tableau still optimal? We analyse this by looking at the dual tableau. We must see whether the first 3 values in the C-row are still non-positive. Now these values will be

$$(56 + \Delta) \times 3/7 + 105 \times (-2/7) = -6 + 3\Delta/7$$

$$(56 + \Delta) \times (-5/7) + 105 \times 1/7 = -25 - 5\Delta/7$$

$$(56 + \Delta) \times (-1) + 105 \times 1 - 56 = -7 - \Delta$$

It follows that the values will remain non-positive as long as $\Delta \leqslant 6 \times 7/3 = 14$. We can increase the availability of 56 to 70, at a price of 13/7 per unit, without losing by this transaction. If we bought more, the tableau would cease to be optimal, and we would have to perform at least one more iteration, which would reduce the value of the objective function. From this new value we could then deduce how much we might pay for a larger purchase than 14 units.

An analogous calculation, referring to raw material R_2, reveals that the increase must not exceed 7 units, if we pay 3/7 per unit.

It is obvious, that all necessary calculations can be carried out from the x-tableau, and that the y-tableau need not be written down explicitly.

(b) Introducing a new constraint

We show our approach again by an example. Suppose we started from the problem maximize

$$4x_1 + 5x_2$$

subject to

$$4x_1 + x_2 \leqslant 56$$

$$5x_1 + 3x_2 \leqslant 105$$

(Example 1.1 without the third constraint) and obtain the tableaus

	x_1	x_2			x_3	x_2	
B	-4	-5	0	B	1	-4	56
x_3	4^*	1	56	x_1	1/4	1/4	14
x_4	5	3	105	x_4	$-5/4$	$7/4^*$	35

	x_3	x_4			x_1	x_4	
B	$-13/7$	16/7	136	B	13/3	5/3	175
x_1	$3/7^*$	$-1/7$	9	x_3	7/3	$-1/3$	21
x_2	$-5/7$	4/7	20	x_2	5/3	1/3	35

Now we wish to add a further constraint

$$x_1 + 2x_2 \leqslant 56$$

The values $x_1 = 0, x_2 = 35$ do not satisfy it.

From the last tableau we have

$$x_2 + 5x_1/3 + x_4/3 = 35$$

so that the new constraint in terms of the last non-basic variables is

$$x_1 + 2(35 - 5x_1/3 - x_4/3) \leqslant 56$$

or, introducing x_5 as a slack variable

$$-7x_1/3 - 2x_4/3 + x_5 = -14$$

We add this to the last tableau

	x_1	x_4	
B	13/3	5/3	175
x_3	7/3	−1/3	21
x_2	5/3	1/3	35
x_5	−7/3	−2/3	−14

We continue by the Dual Simplex Method, to obtain

	x_5	x_4	
B	13/7	3/7	149
x_3	1	−1	7
x_2	5/7	−1/7	25
x_1	−3/7	2/7	6

The result is, of course, that of Example 1.1.

The Duality Theorem can serve as a starting point for the proof of other theorems. As an example, we prove the theorem of Farkas [4] as follows.

Theorem 3.1

If for all solutions of $Ax \geqslant 0$ we have also $a'x \geqslant 0$, then there exists a vector $y \geqslant 0$ such that $a = A'y$. A is an m by n matrix, x and a are n-vectors, and y is an m-vector.

Proof

Consider the two dual problems:

minimize $a'x$ maximize $0'y$

subject to   subject to

    $Ax \geqslant 0$ $A'y = a, y \geqslant 0$

If for all x which satisfy $Ax \geqslant 0$ the inequality $a'x$ is also true, then the minimum of $a'x$ is zero, attainable by $x = 0$ which satisfies $Ax \geqslant 0$. Then the dual has also a solution, i.e. some $y \geqslant 0$ exists for which $A'y = a$.

The theorem of Farkas can be re-phrased as a 'theorem of alternatives'. Either $A'y = a$, $y \geqslant 0$ has a solution, or $Ax \geqslant 0, a'x < 0$ has a solution (note that both these cases cannot hold at the same time, because $y \geqslant 0$ and $Ax \geqslant 0$, then $y'Ax \geqslant 0$, and if $A'y = a$, so that $a' = y'A$, then $a'x = y'Ax \geqslant 0$, but not < 0).

If we replace A' by (A', I_n), and y' by (y', t'), where I_n is the n by n identity matrix and t is an n-vector, then we obtain the corollary either

    $A'y + I_n t = a, y \geqslant 0, t \geqslant 0$

i.e.

    $A'y \leqslant a, y \geqslant 0$

has a solution y, or

    $Ax \geqslant 0, x \geqslant 0, a'x < 0$

has a solution x. The additional requirement $x \geqslant 0$ which appears here has changed the equations $A'y = a$ into inequalities $A'y \leqslant a$.

We have derived the theorem of Farkas from the Duality Theorem. It is also possible to derive the Duality Theorem from the theorem of Farkas assuming, of course, that the latter has been proved independently, but we do not expand on this possibility here.

If, in the corollary to the theorem of Farkas, we replace A by $(A, -e)$, where e is an n-vector whose components are all unity, and replace a by

$$\begin{pmatrix} 0 \\ \cdot \\ \cdot \\ \cdot \\ 0 \\ -1 \end{pmatrix}$$

then we obtain the alternatives either

$$A'y \leqslant 0, -e'y \leqslant -1, y \geqslant 0$$

has a solution y, or

$$Ax - ze \geqslant 0, x \geqslant 0, z \geqslant 0, -z < 0$$

has a solution x, z, where z is a scalar. This can be written either

$$A'y \leqslant 0, y \geqslant 0$$

but not $y = 0$ has a solution y, or

$$Ax > 0, x \geqslant 0$$

but not $x = 0$ has a solution x (notice that $y \geqslant 0$, but not $= 0$ means that some of the components of y may be zero, but not all of them). This leads to the following theorem.

Theorem 3.2
At least one of two dual problems must have an unbounded feasible region, unless neither has a feasible region.

Proof
(a) Let only one of two dual problems have a feasible region. Because the other problem has no feasible region, the solution to the first must be infinite, by the Duality Theorem. This is only possible if the feasible region is unbounded.

(b) Let $Ax \geqslant b$, $x \geqslant 0$ have a solution $x^{(\prime)}$, and let $A'y \leqslant c, y \geqslant 0$ have the solution $y^{(\prime)}$. The system $A'y \leqslant 0, y \geqslant 0$, but not $= 0$ may have a solution y^0 (case i), or it may have no solution (case ii).

In case (i) the system $A'(y^{(\prime)} + \lambda y^0) \leqslant c$ for all $\lambda > 0$, and hence its feasible region is unbounded.

In case (ii) the system $Ax \geqslant 0, x \geqslant 0$, but not $= 0$ has a solution x^0, and $A(x^{(\prime)} + \lambda x^0) \geqslant b$ for all $\lambda > 0$. Once more the feasible region is unbounded.

In Example 3.1 it was the minimizing problem which had an unbounded feasible region (see Fig. 1.2). This does not mean, of course, that its optimal solution was infinite.

As a final example in this chapter we prove the theorem of Hall [8].

Let m sets $S_j = (s_{1,j}, s_{2,j}, \ldots, s_{n_j,j})$, $(j = 1, \ldots, m)$ be given.

There may be different sets containing the same item. It is required to find an item from each set, its 'representative', different sets having different representatives. Such a system is called a *system of distinct representatives* (SDR). The theorem we prove states the following.

Theorem 3.3
It is possible to find a system of district representatives if and only if any k sets out of the m given sets $(k = 1, \ldots, m)$ contain at least k different items between them.

Proof
The necessity of the condition is obvious. We prove its sufficiency by an application of the concept of duality [10].

Introduce constants $a_{i,j}(i = 1, \ldots, n; j = 1, \ldots, m)$ and let $a_{i,j} = 1$ if $s_{i,j}$ is an item in S_j, and $a_{i,j} = 0$ otherwise. Also, introduce $x_{i,j} = 1$ if $s_{i,j}$ is chosen as representative of S_j and equals 0 otherwise. If we have a system of distinct representatives, then

$$(*) \sum_{j=1}^{m} x_{i,j} \leqslant 1$$

for all i, and

$$(**) \sum_{i=1}^{n} x_{i,j} \leqslant 1$$

for all j.

The number of representatives in the system will be

$$\sum_{j=1}^{m} \sum_{i=1}^{n} a_{i,j} x_{i,j} = B$$

say. If all sets are represented, then $B = m$, otherwise it is less than m. We ask if B can be made equal to m: we want to maximize B subject to the conditions above, and if it cannot be made equal to m, then we want to find out why.

This is a linear programming problem. It is, in fact, a very special case of the *Assignment Problem*, which is mentioned in Chapter 5.

We introduce dual variables u_i, corresponding to (*), and v_j

corresponding to (**). The dual problem reads minimize

$$\sum_i u_i + \sum_j v_j$$

subject to $u_i + v_j \geqslant a_{i,j}$ (all i and j), $u_i \geqslant 0$, $v_j \geqslant 0$ (all i and j). The u_i and v_j will be either 0 or 1, and if $a_{i,j} = 1$, then at least one of u_i and v_j must be 1. We want to minimize the number of those u_i and v_j which equal 1.

Suppose the problem has been solved, and the numbers of the u_i and of the v_j which are 0 or 1, are as follows:

	u_i	v_j
1	t	$m - k$
0	$n - t$	k
	n	m

Then $\Sigma_i u_i + \Sigma_i v_i$, which equals $\Sigma_j \Sigma_j a_{i,j} x_{i,j}$ by the Duality Theorem, equals $m - k + t$. This is less than m (i.e. we could not find a complete SDR) when $t < k$. We want to find the reason for this.

Let the k sets for which $v_j = 0$ be these

$S_1 \quad s_{i_1 1}, s_{i_2 1}, \ldots,$

.   .   .

.   .   .

.   .   .

$S_k \quad s_{r_1 k}, s_{r_2 k}, \ldots,$

and hence the $a_{i,j}$ with the same subscripts is 1. Of course, there may be the same item in more than one set.

Now, if $v_1 = 0, \ldots, v_k = 0$, then all of $u_{i_1}, u_{i_2}, \ldots, u_{r_1}, u_{r_2}, \ldots$ must equal 1, and there cannot be more of these than t. Consequently, the k sets for which $v_j = 0$ cannot have more than $t < k$ items $s_{i,j}$ between them.

It follows that, if any k sets have k or more different items between them, then an SDR of the m sets exists.

Problems

3.1. Formulate and solve the problems which are dual to Problem 2.1 parts (a) and (b).

3.2. Solve the dual to Problem 2.6.

CHAPTER 4

Theory of games

The theory of games deals with decision problems in situations where the outcome depends not merely on a decision taken by one person, but also on decisions of others, who might be deliberate or accidental, known or unknown opponents. Parlour games are an obvious model of such situations.

We shall not deal here with the very wide scope of the theory and of its various extensions and applications, but only with that part of the theory which is related to the concept of duality. We consider only games between two persons, when each player has a finite number of choices, where each player makes one single choice — not a succession of them — and where the outcome depends on the simultaneous choices of the adversaries in such a way that one loses what the other gains. The last mentioned fact can be expressed by saying that the sum of the gains of the two opponents is zero.

We deal, then, with finite, two-person, zero-sum games and we shall not enter into the theory of infinite games or of non-zero-sum games.

The games we shall be dealing with are also called matrix games, because their rules can be completely described by a 'pay-off matrix', an example of which follows.

Example 4.1

Player B's choices

Player A's choices
$$
\begin{pmatrix}
 & b_1 & b_2 & b_3 \\
a_1 & 3 & 0 & -1 \\
a_2 & 2 & 1 & 2 \\
a_3 & -1 & 0 & 3
\end{pmatrix}
$$

Each element of the table (matrix) is the result of simultaneous choices by A and B, quoting the gain of A and (hence) the loss to B. Which choice should A make?

If A chooses a_1, then the worst that could happen to him is that B had chosen b_3, because then the pay-off to him, A, will be the smallest in the row of a_1, namely, -1. If A chooses a_2 (or a_3), he must fear that B chooses b_2 (or b_1). B argues in a similar way, and he is concerned with the maxima in the various columns.

According to the spirit of the theory of games, A will look for the largest of the row minima, for the 'maximin'. Hence he will choose a_2. B will look for the smallest of the column maxima, the 'minimax', and will choose b_2. The outcome, the 'value' of the game, will be a payment of 1 from B to A.

Suppose that when all this is settled, a player wonders whether he could have done better if he had known the choice of his opponent. Both A and B will find, in this case, that they could not have done better; neither of the players will regret his choice with hindsight. This is so because the value in the intersection of the chosen row and the chosen column is the smallest in its row, and at the same time the largest in its column. By an obvious geometric analogy, we call its position a *saddle point*.

This settles the case when there is a saddle point in the pay-off matrix, i.e. when the maximin equals the minimax. However often the players repeat this game, they will always make the same choices. But what if there is no saddle point, as in the following example.

Example 4.2

	b_1	b_2	b_3
a_1	1	-1	3
a_2	3	5	-3
a_3	6	2	-2

Here all player A can be sure of is to lose not more than $\max(-1, -3, -2) = -1$, by choosing a_1, and player B can be sure of not losing more than $\min(6, 5, 3) = 3$, by choosing b_3. There is no saddle point in this table.

If we want to find choices which are 'best', in some sense, we must look for some new criterion. We remember that in a game with saddle point the players are well advised to stick to their respective choices, however often they repeat the game. In the present case there is no reason for this. In fact, it is even advisable to change one's choices from game to game, in a random manner, lest the opponent guess what one is choosing. Let us see what can happen in such a case.

For the sake of the argument, assume that A chooses, in the long run, a_1 twice out of three times, a_2 once out of three times, but never a_3. Assume, also, that B chooses b_2 and b_3 equally often, but never b_1. We call this type of decision a 'mixed strategy', as distinct from a 'pure strategy', always making the same choice.

If A makes his choice as above, and B chooses b_1 (A does not know that B has decided never to do this), then he can expect to gain, in the long run, on average,

$$2/3 \times 1 + 1/3 \times 3 = 5/3$$

If B chose b_2 (or b_3), A gains, on average

$$2/3 \times (-1) + 1/3 \times 5 = 1 \ (or \ 2/3 \times 3 + 1/3 \times (-3) = 1).$$

The smallest of these expectations — we repeat on average, in the long run — is min $(5/3, 1, 1) = 1$.

This was calculated assuming that B chose his first, or his second or his third strategy, but if he mixes his strategies, the outcome can, in any case, not be smaller than 1.

From Bs point of view, the argument runs as follows.

If A chooses a_1 B loses on average $\frac{1}{2} \times (-1) + \frac{1}{2} \times 3 = 1$

a_2 $\qquad\qquad\qquad\qquad\qquad$ $\frac{1}{2} \times 5 + \frac{1}{2}(-3) = 1$

a_3 $\qquad\qquad\qquad\qquad\qquad$ $\frac{1}{2} \times 2 + \frac{1}{2} \times (-2) = 0$

The largest of these values, max$(1, 1, 0) = 1$. The expectations of the two players are equal numerically, although A wins and B loses that amount. If they had chosen different mixed strategies, or indeed a pure one, the result might have been different.

We say now that, because the two optimal average pay-offs are numerically equal, the mixed strategies which the players have chosen are the best strategies available to them.

Indeed, if A can be certain that with his strategy he will win at least 1, whatever B does, then the best B can do is not to let A win more, and if B can be certain that with his own strategy he can not lose more than 1, whatever A does, then the best A can do is not to let B lose less.

On scrutinizing the result in more detail, we notice that both players are better off than if they had chosen a pure strategy, A, by having a guarantee of winning at least 1, against not losing more than 1, and B by having a guarantee of not losing more than 1 against not losing more than 3.

In Example 4.2 it was possible to make the two expectations numerically equal. Thus, in the sense we have explained, best strategies could be found. It is, therefore, of interest to know if there exist strategies which always lead to numerically equal average expectations for both players, whatever the pay-off matrix.

We shall now show that such strategies always exist, and at the same time we shall see how such best strategies can be computed.

Let the pay-off matrix be

$$\begin{pmatrix} a_{1,1} \cdots a_{1,m} \\ a_{2,1} \cdots a_{2,m} \\ \cdot \quad \cdot \\ \cdot \quad \cdot \\ \cdot \quad \cdot \\ a_{n,1} \cdots a_{n,m} \end{pmatrix}$$

Some of the $a_{i,j}$ may be negative or zero. However, if we add a constant c to all $a_{i,j}$, the optimal strategies are not affected. This may be seen by imagining that B pays to A an amount c before the game starts, and then they play the game. The advantages or disadvantages of any decisions during this latter stage remain unaffected by the initial payment.

We may therefore assume, for the computation of strategies, that the $a_{i,j}$ are all positive. The value of the game will be less by c than that value which is obtained after having added c to $a_{i,j}$.

If A decides his mixed strategy to be $(x_1, \ldots, x_n)$, i.e. choosing rows in proportions x_i, then he obtains

$$\sum_{i=1}^{n} a_{i,j} x_i$$

when B chooses column j.

If we write v for

$$\min_{j} \sum_{i=1}^{n} a_{i,j} x_i$$

then

$$a_{1,j}x_1 + \cdots + a_{n,j}x_n \geqslant v \ (j = 1, \ldots, m)$$

Also

$$x_1 + \cdots + x_n = 1$$

and

$$x_1 \geqslant 0, \ldots, x_n \geqslant 0$$

The unknown v is to be made as large as possible by the choice of x_i.

We have assumed that all $a_{i,j}$ are positive. Then v will certainly also be positive. We introduce new variables $X_i = x_i/v$, and have the following problem.

Maximize v, i.e. minimize $\sum_{i=1}^{n} X_i$ (which equals $1/v$) subject to

$$\sum_{i=1}^{n} a_{i,j} X_i \geqslant 1$$

$$X_i \geqslant 0 \ (i = 1, \ldots, n) \tag{P_1}$$

Now look at player Bs problem. He chooses $y_1, \ldots, y_m$ so that

$$\sum_{j=1}^{m} a_{i,j} y_j \leqslant w \ (i = 1, \ldots, n)$$

$$y_1 + \cdots + y_m = 1$$

$$y_j \geqslant 0 \text{ for all } j,$$

and he wishes to minimize

$$\max_i \sum_{j=1}^{m} a_{i,j} y_j$$

which we have called w.

If we introduce $Y_j = y_j/w$, then we obtain the following problem. Maximize

$$\sum_{j=1}^{m} Y_j \quad \text{(which equals } 1/w)$$

subject to

$$\sum_{j=1}^{m} a_{i,j} Y_j \leqslant 1$$

$$Y_j \geqslant 0 \; (j = 1, \ldots, m) \tag{P_2}$$

(P_1) and (P_2) are dual problems. Therefore the two optimal values, the minimum of $1/v$ and the maximum of $1/w$, are equal. So are, therefore, the largest v and the smallest w.

The average pay-offs for A and for B are numerically equal, if they choose, respectively, $x_i = X_i v$ and $y_j = Y_j w$, given by the solution of (P_1) and (P_2). These strategies are best in the sense which we have explained.

Of course, to find these strategies, we need not solve both problems, because the shadow costs in (P_1) are the values of the variables in (P_2), and vice versa.

As an illustration, we take Example 4.2 again. First, we add $c = 4$ to the values in the pay-off table, to make them all positive.

5	3	7
7	9	1
10	6	2

It is then convenient to formulate (P_2), because we can then start with the slack variables, of value 1, as basic variables and we have then merely to copy the rows of the pay-off table into the left hand sides of the constraints. Because we keep the dual relationship in mind, we use now the subscripts 4, 5, and 6 for Y_j. The problem is then maximize

$$B = Y_4 + Y_5 + Y_6$$

subject to

$$5Y_4 + 3Y_5 + 7Y_6 \leqslant 1$$
$$7Y_4 + 9Y_5 + Y_6 \leqslant 1$$
$$10Y_4 + 6Y_5 + 2Y_6 \leqslant 1$$
$$Y_4, Y_5, Y_6 \geqslant 0$$

The final tableau will be

	Y_1	Y_2	Y_4	
B	2/15	1/15	2/15	1/5
Y_5	−1/60	7/60	11/15	1/10
Y_6	3/20	−1/20	2/5	1/10
Y_3	−1/5	−3/5	18/5	1/5

so that

$$Y_1 = 0, Y_2 = 0, Y_3 = 1/5, Y_4 = 0, Y_5 = 1/10, Y_6 = 1/10$$

and

$$X_1 = 2/15, X_2 = 1/15, X_3 = 0, X_4 = 2/15, X_5 = 0, X_6 = 0$$

Then $1/w = Y_4 + Y_5 + Y_6 = 1/5$, $w = 5$, hence

$$y_4 = 0, y_5 = 1/10 \times 5 = \tfrac{1}{2}, y_6 = 1/10 \times 5 = \tfrac{1}{2}$$

Also $1/v = X_1 + X_2 + X_3 = 1/5, v = 5$, hence

$$x_1 = 2/15 \times 5 = 2/3, x_2 = 1/15 \times 5 = 1/3, x_3 = 0$$

We had added 4 to the pay-offs, therefore the value of the game is $v - 4 = w - 4 = 1$. These results are those which we have found earlier.

This way of solving a game also shows that the number of active strategies is the same for both players. We started off with the slack variables in problems (P_2) as basic variables, and the subscripts of the non-basic variables corresponded to those of the slack variables in problem (P_1). After each iteration the number of basic variables with subscripts of non-slack variables in (P_2) equals the number of non-basic variables with subscripts of non-slack variables in (P_1). There are as many values of the one as there are shadow costs of the other. Of course, in exceptional cases such a value may be zero. We would then still call the corresponding strategy active, with a qualification.

Having reached the result in Example 4.2, we see that player A could have ignored his third strategy altogether (although he could not know this to begin with). The game could then have been defined by the pay-off matrix

$$\begin{pmatrix} 1 & -1 & 3 \\ 3 & 5 & -3 \end{pmatrix}$$

Such a game with two rows can be given a simple geometric representation. We mark off the values corresponding to As strategies on
verticals, as in Fig. 4.1, and we draw lines connecting the values in
the same column, as 'strategy lines' of B. Any choice of A can be
marked off on the base line I–II of length 1. Any point at a distance
d from I, and hence at a distance $1 - d$ from II marks a mixture of
strategies with ratios $1 - d$ times the strategy of the first row and d
times the strategy of the second row. Perpendicularly above that
point any strategy line of B has the height which indicates the
payment to A, if B chooses that strategy of his. In our example, the

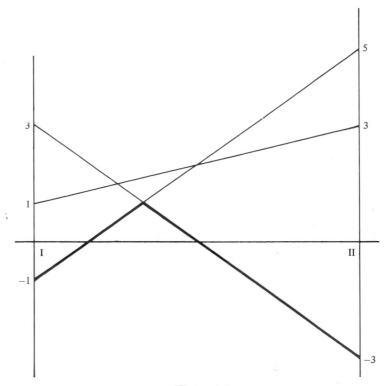

Figure 4.1

height of the first strategy line above the strategy point $(1 - d) : d$ of A is

$$(1 - d) \times 1 + d \times 3$$

that of the second strategy line is

$$(1 - d) \times (-1) + d \times 5$$

and that of the third is

$$(1 - d) \times 3 + d \times (-3)$$

For each choice of d, A can determine the smallest value which he can obtain, dependent on Bs choice of his strategy. He will therefore choose d so as to make the smallest value as high as possible. This he does by choosing $d = 1/3$, and the height of the lowest line above this point is 1, the value of the game.

It is easily seen how a diagram can be drawn when it is the minimizing player who has two strategies.

A game where one player who has three strategies, and his opponent has at least three strategies, can be represented by a three-dimensional model. Fig. 4.2 shows models of the game in Example 4.2 both from As and Bs point of view.

We mention an amusing application of the theory of games to the question of how to bet on a racecourse. The theory of games has no suggestion to offer to the inveterate gambler, or to somebody with inside information, but only to the casual player.

There are n horses, with odds a_i to 1 on horse i. If you stake x_i on this horse, and it wins, you receive your stake back; if it loses, you lose your stake. How should you divide an amount of 1 between bets on the n horses?

If horse 1 wins, you win $\quad a_1 x_1 - x_2 \quad - \cdots - x_n$

$\qquad\qquad 2 \qquad\qquad\qquad\quad -x_1 + a_2 x_2 - \cdots - x_n$

$\qquad\qquad \cdot \qquad\qquad\qquad\qquad \cdot \qquad \cdot \qquad\quad \cdot$

$\qquad\qquad \cdot \qquad\qquad\qquad\qquad \cdot \qquad \cdot \qquad\quad \cdot$

$\qquad\qquad \cdot \qquad\qquad\qquad\qquad \cdot \qquad \cdot \qquad\quad \cdot$

$\qquad\qquad n \qquad\qquad\qquad\quad -x_1 - x_2 \quad - \cdots + a_n x_n$

Because $x_1 + x_2 + \cdots + x_n = 1$, the ith line can be written

$$a_i x_i + x_i - 1 = c_i x_i - 1$$

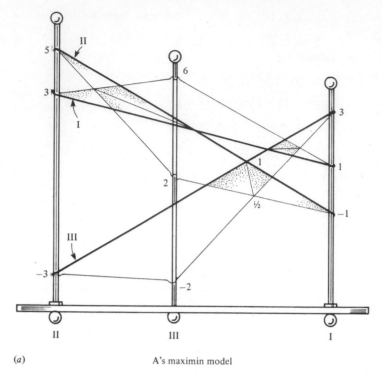

(a)   A's maximin model

Figure 4.2a

say. If the smallest possible gain should be as large as possible, we have to maximize v subject to

$$c_i x_i - 1 \geqslant v \ (i = 1, \ldots, n)$$

subject to

$$\sum_{i=1}^{n} x_i = 1, x_i \geqslant 0$$

The value v has $c_i x_i - 1$ as upper bound. It will be largest if all $c_i x_i$ are equal; if they are not, then the value of v would be depressed, because at least one of the $c_i x_i - 1$ would be smaller than if they were all equal, in view of

$$\sum_{i=1}^{n} x_i = 1$$

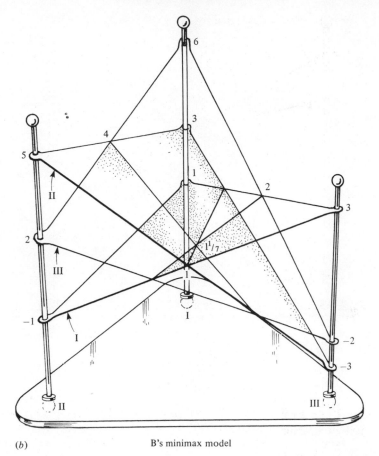

(b)   B's minimax model

Figure 4.2b

Formally, this can be seen as follows. $c_i(x_i + \delta_i) - 1$ differs from $c_i x_i - 1$ by $c_i \delta_i$, but

$$\sum_{i=1}^{n} \delta_i = 0,$$

and $c_i > 0$, so that not all δ_i can be positive, and the smallest $c_i(x_i + \delta_i) - 1$ is smaller than $c_i x_i - 1$.

We have therefore to solve

$$c_i x_i = c_1 x_1 \; (i = 2, \ldots, n)$$
$$x_1 + \cdots + x_n = 1$$

These conditions are satisfied by

$$x_i = k/c_i \quad (i = 1, \ldots, n)$$

where k is given by

$$\sum_{i=1}^{n} x_i = k \sum_{i=1}^{n} 1/c_i = 1$$

Then

$$v = c_i x_i - 1 = k - 1 = \left(1 - \sum_{i=1}^{n} 1/c_i \right) \Bigg/ \sum_{i=1}^{n} 1/c_i$$

If we make the suggested choice

$$x_i = (1/c_i) \Bigg/ \sum_{i=1}^{n} 1/c_i$$

then the gain is $v = k - 1$, a constant, whichever horse wins.

Naturally, we shall want this amount to be positive. We would not bet if we knew that we are bound to lose, whichever horse wins. Now $v > 0$ if

$$\sum_{i=1}^{n} 1/c_i = \sum_{i=1}^{n} \frac{1}{a_i + 1} < 1$$

where $a_i:1$ are the odds on horse i.

If you watch the book-makers' boards on a racecourse, you will find, as a rule, that the condition just given is not satisfied. But it has been reported that once, for a short time, a gambler would have won at the 1954 Grand National in Aintree if he had spotted the advantage from the odds — and if he had known our theory!

Problems

4.1. Player A chooses the number 2 or 4, B chooses two numbers out of 1, 2, 4. A loses the total of numbers chosen by both, and he wins the total of numbers chosen only by one of them. Which numbers should they choose, and which entry fee should A or B pay to make the game fair?

4.2. The game of 'Two-finger Morra' is played as follows. There are two players, A and B. Each player shows either one or two fingers, and at the same time he shouts his guess of the number of fingers the other player shows. If both guess correctly, or if both guess wrongly, no payment is made. The single player who guesses correctly, receives the sum of the numbers of fingers shown. Find the optimal strategies of the players and the pay-off.

CHAPTER 5

Transportation and flow in networks

We have seen a number of quite sophisticated algorithms for the solution of linear programming problems. We shall now look at problems which are, in fact, of linear programming type, but which have structures that enable us to solve them in a much simpler way than by applying methods appropriate to the general form.

One of these problems is the *Transportation Problem* [9]. Let a_i units of goods be situated in n different places $P_1, \ldots, P_n$ and let b_j of the $\Sigma_i a_i$ units be required in m different places $Q_1, \ldots, Q_m$. Let also $\Sigma_i a_i = \Sigma_j b_j$.

We know, for each pair (i, j), the cost $c_{i,j}$ of transporting one unit from P_i to Q_j. It is required to find the redistribution of goods at the smallest total cost. We can formulate this problem as follows.

Let $x_{i,j}$ be the number of units sent from P_i to Q_j. From each P_i we send goods to the various Q_j, and

$$x_{i,1} + \cdots + x_{i,m} = a_i (i = 1, \ldots, n) \tag{5.1}$$

In each of Q_j there arrive goods from the various P_i, and

$$x_{1,j} + \cdots + x_{n,j} = b_j (j = 1, \ldots, m) \tag{5.2}$$

The cost of the redistribution is

$$\sum_{i=1}^{n} \sum_{j=1}^{m} c_{i,j} x_{i,j} = C$$

and this amount is to be minimized. Of course, $x_{i,j} \geqslant 0$ for all i and j, and we have a linear programming problem where the constraints are equations.

This problem, with its special pattern of coefficients, can be solved by a special method [6] which we describe now by an example.

Example 5.1

Let the a_i, b_j and $c_{i,j}$ be as follows

a_1	a_2		b_1	b_2	b_3
4	5		1	5	3

$$c_{i,j}$$

	$j =$	1	2	3
$i =$	1	4	5	7
	2	7	10	8

We start by determining $x_{1,1}$. It cannot be larger than $a_1 (= 4)$, or $b_1 (= 1)$, so we make it 1. The remaining units to be redistributed are then

column totals

		b_2	b_3
	$a_1 - 1$	$x_{1,2}$	$x_{1,3}$
row totals			
	a_2	$x_{2,2}$	$x_{2,3}$

The b_1 column has been exhausted, but not the a_1 row, so we look for $x_{1,2}$. It cannot be larger than 3, and this exhausts the a_1 row. The remaining units are

	$b_2 - 3$	b_3
a_2	$x_{2,2}$	$x_{2,3}$

Now $x_{2,2} = 2$ (which exhausts column b_2) and $x_{2,3} = 3$ which exhausts, finally, the a_2 row as well as the b_3 column. The solution which we have found is

column totals

		1	5	3
	4	1	3	
row totals				
	5		2	3

The rows as well as the columns add up to their marginal totals, hence this is a solution. We are now asking whether this is a basic solution. It is easily seen that our procedure will produce (not more than) $m + n - 1$ positive $x_{i,j}$. Now we have $m + n$ constraints, but only $m + n - 1$ are independent, because

$$\sum_{i=1}^{n} a_i = \sum_{i=1}^{n} \sum_{j=1}^{m} x_{i,j} = \sum_{j=1}^{m} b_j$$

which shows that any one of the equations is redundant — it can be reconstructed from the others, and hence does not add any new information to them.

The above solution is therefore basic and feasible. The question remains whether it is optimal.

To answer this question, we make use of the Duality Theorem. We introduce dual variables $u_1, \ldots, u_n$ corresponding to the constraints of Equations (5.1) and $v_1, \ldots, v_m$ corresponding to those of Equation (5.2). The fact that one of the constraints is redundant means that we can choose the value of one of these variables arbitrarily. For convenience, we make it zero.

The dual system is maximize

$$\sum_i a_i u_i + \sum_j b_j v_j$$

subject to

$$u_i + v_j \leqslant c_{i,j}$$

for all i and j, u_i and v_j not restricted in sign.

The principle of complementary slackness demands that if $x_{i,j} > 0$, then $u_i + v_j = c_{i,j}$. We determine therefore values for u_i and v_j which satisfy these equations for those i and j for which $x_{i,j} > 0$. This is easily done when one of them has been made equal to zero (or to any other arbitrarily chosen value). Then we test whether the other u_i and v_j satisfy the condition $u_i + v_j \leqslant c_{i,j}$. If we find a pair for which this does not hold, i.e. a pair such that $u_i + v_j > c_{i,j}$, then that corresponding $x_{i,j}$ (which, at this stage, has value zero), can be made positive with advantage, thereby reducing $\Sigma_i \Sigma_j c_{i,j} x_{i,j}$.

We do this in our example. We must make $u_i + v_j = c_{i,j}$ for (i, j) equal to $(1, 1)$, $(1, 2)$, $(2, 2)$ and $(2, 3)$, because it was in these cells where we entered positive values. We first make $u_1 = 0$. We have then, repeating the table of the $c_{i,j}$,

	$c_{i,j}$			u_i
	4	5	7	0
	7	10	8	5
v_j	4	5	3	

Now looking at the cells where $x_{i,j} = 0$, we find $4 + 5 > 7 (= c_{2,1})$ and $3 + 0 < 7 (= c_{1,3})$. It is therefore useful to make $x_{2,1}$ positive, but not $x_{1,3}$. The question is then which of the positive (basic) $x_{i,j}$ to make zero instead.

The exchange must be such that the marginal totals are not disturbed by the new values of the variables. If we increase $x_{2,1}$, we must decrease $x_{2,2}$ or $x_{2,3}$. If we decreased $x_{2,3}$, we would have to increase $x_{1,3}$, but we do not want to increase more than one of the variables which are now zero (non-basic), because we want to have only basic solutions.

If we decrease $x_{2,2}$, we must increase $x_{1,2}$, then as a consequence decrease $x_{1,1}$ ($x_{1,3}$ cannot be decreased, because it is already 0) and this makes up for the increase of $x_{2,1}$.

We see that our wish to consider only basic solutions prescribes that we must, starting from the variables to be made basic, find a circuit of alternately horizontal and vertical steps, using as vertices of the circuit only occupied positions, as it were, as stepping stones.

We quote again the basic solution which we have found and indicate the circuit by + and − labels, indicating increases and decreases.

	1	5	3
4	1−	3+	
5	+	2−	3

How far can we increase $x_{2,1}$? We must not make any of the other variables negative as a consequence. We find the smallest value which has a − label against it, in our case 1, and this is the amount which can be subtracted and added alternately along the circuit. We obtain

$x_{i,j}$					$c_{i,j}$			u_i
	1	5	3					
4		4			4	5	7	0
5	1	1	3		7	10	8	5
v_j					2	5	3	

Now $0 + 2 < 4 (= c_{1,1})$, and $0 + 3 < 7 (= c_{1,3})$, and we have reached the final answer (see Fig. 5.1). The total cost is $4 \times 5 + 1 \times 7 + 1 \times 10 + 3 \times 8 = 61$. By duality, this is equal to $\Sigma_i a_i u_i + \Sigma_j b_j v_j$, which is $5 \times 5 + 2 \times 1 + 5 \times 5 + 3 \times 3 = 61$.

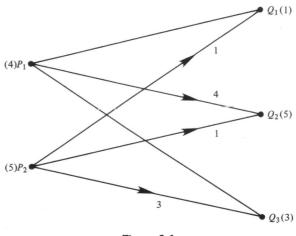

Figure 5.1

It might not always be so easy to find a circuit as it was in this example, but a circuit will always exist. It may be more involved, though, than in the simple case above and could, for instance, in a larger problem, look as in Fig. 5.2.

The procedure which we have mentioned does not involve any division. If we start with integer values for a_i and b_j, $x_{i,j}$ will all be integers. Thus, if the problem concerns the redistribution of ships,

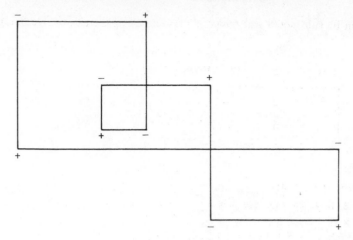

Figure 5.2

for instance, we shall not be in the embarrassing position that we are told to send fractions of a ship on different routes.

It is possible that $u_i + v_j = c_{ij}$ for a pair (i, j) for which $x_{i,j} = 0$, as for instance in the following case.

		$x_{i,j}$					$c_{i,j}$		u_i
	1	5	3						
4		4–	+			4	5	3	0
5	1	1+	3–			7	10	8	5
					v_j	2	5	3	

where we have changed the cost of $x_{1,3}$ from 7 to 3. Now $u_1 + v_3 = 3 = c_{1,3}$. If we wish, we can introduce $x_{1,3}$, with circuit as indicated, and obtain

		$x_{i,j}$	
	1	5	3
4		1	3
5	1	4	

The cost is 61, as before; the a_i, b_j, u_i, v_j have not changed. This is a case of multiple solutions, with a zero shadow cost. We can combine two optimal solutions, using positive weights which add up to unity, e.g. $\frac{1}{2}$ and $\frac{1}{2}$, which would produce

$$x_{i,j}$$

	1	5	3
4		$2\frac{1}{2}$	$1\frac{1}{2}$
5	1	$2\frac{1}{2}$	$1\frac{1}{2}$

Then we cannot expect the values of $x_{i,j}$ to be integers, although some combination might have this property, for instance, if we used weights 2/3 and 1/3, which produces

	1	5	3
4		2	2
5	1	3	1

or weights 1/3 and 2/3, which produces

	1	5	3
4		3	1
5	1	2	2

We must also mention the case of degeneracy, when 'too many' x_{ij} are zero, i.e. when a basic variable also has this value. In fact, our original Example 5.1 could have been written as follows

$$c_{ij}$$

	5	1	3
5	10	7	8
4	5	4	7

by exchanging the subscripts of the places of availability P_1 and P_2, and also those of the places of requirement Q_1 and Q_2, which plainly would not have changed the problem. We would then have chosen 5 for x_{11}, thereby exhausting the first row as well as the first column. We would have started again with

$$
\begin{array}{c|cc}
 & 1 & 3 \\
\hline
4 & 1 & 3 \\
\end{array}
$$

which gives the basic solutions

$$
\begin{array}{ccc}
 & x_{ij} & \\
 & 5 \quad 1 \quad 3 \\
\hline
5 & 5 \\
4 & 0 \quad 1 \quad 3 \\
\end{array}
\qquad
\begin{array}{ccc}
 & x_{ij} & \\
 & 5 \quad 1 \quad 3 \\
\hline
5 & 5 \quad 0 \\
4 & \quad 1 \quad 3 \\
\end{array}
$$

To determine the u_i and v_j in such a case (we need them to see if we have already reached the best solution), we must act as if only the row (or only the column) had been dealt with and that a 0 delivery still remains in the column (or in the row). This allows us to continue, for instance, with

$$
\begin{array}{c|ccc|c}
 & 5 & 1 & 3 & u_i \\
\hline
5 & 5 & & & \\
4 & 0 & 1 & 3 & -5 \\
\hline
v_j & 10 & 9 & 12 & \\
\end{array}
\qquad
\begin{array}{c|ccc|c}
 & 5 & 1 & 3 & u_i \\
\hline
5 & 2 & 3 & & \\
4 & 3 & 1 & & -5 \\
\hline
v_j & 10 & 9 & 8 & \\
\end{array}
\qquad
\begin{array}{c|ccc|c}
 & 5 & 1 & 3 & u_i \\
\hline
5 & 1 & 1 & 3 & \\
4 & 4 & & & -5 \\
\hline
v_j & 10 & 7 & 8 & \\
\end{array}
$$

and this is the same answer as before.

The problem which could be called 'most degenerate' is the *Assignment Problem* [3]. It deals with the question of how to assign n persons to n jobs, when their suitabilities for these jobs, expressed numerically, are known. This can be formulated as a transportation problem, with all availabilities 1 (one of the persons in each row) and all requirements 1 (one of the jobs for each column). We want to maximize the total suitability ratings of all persons in those jobs to which they are severally assigned, and in order to keep to the usual transportation model, we call the negatives of the rating values the costs. Clearly, all variables will have value zero or unity.

A very special case of the assignment problem is that where we use only 1 or 0 as merit ratings, i.e. suitability or non-suitability for the several jobs. Naturally, we should like to appoint as many persons as possible to jobs for which they are suited, and we shall hope that this number will be n, or in terms of the formulation, that the cost will be $-n$. Whether this is possible in a given case is, in fact, the question answered by Hall's Theorem, in Chapter 4.

Trans-shipment

We have so far assumed that there are places of departure, P_i, where goods are stored, and places of arrival, Q_j, where goods are required. No traffic was assumed to be possible between two different P_is, or between two different Q_js. However, in reality it might possibly be cheaper to send goods from P_1 to Q_1, say, by sending them first from P_1 to P_2 and then from P_2 to Q_1.

To find out if this is so, we must of course know the cost of transport between any two places of the same type. Let us assume that these costs are as follows, together with the costs between places of different type.

Example 5.3

	P_1	P_2	Q_1	Q_2	Q_3
P_1	0	1	4	5	7
P_2	1	0	7	10	8
Q_1	4	7	0	2	5
Q_2	5	10	2	0	8
Q_3	7	8	5	8	0

We have here a symmetric table, assuming the cost of transport to be independent of direction, but this need not be so. We have also ignored possible trans-shipment from P_i to P_i itself, for instance, harbour costs. If they exist, they would appear in the diagonal of the table.

This looks like a transportation problem, but we are faced with a difficulty. There is nothing required at P_1 or P_2, and nothing is available at any of the Q_j. Therefore, if we used for a_i the values (4, 5, 0, 0, 0), and for b_j the values (0, 0, 1, 5, 3), we would just obtain the same answer as in Example 5.1, with the given costs.

However, this would be wrong, because we see by inspection that, for instance, to send goods from P_2 to Q_1 directly costs 7 per unit, while the route $P_2 \rightarrow P_1 \rightarrow Q_1$ costs only $1 + 4 = 5$ per unit.

To overcome this difficulty, we add to all requirements and to all availabilities a number large enough for possible trans-shipment. The total of all units available would be such a number. In our example, we add 9 to all a_i and to all b_j.

If we solve this as a transportation problem, we obtain

(a)

	9	9	10	14	12
13	7		6		
14	2	9			3
9			4	5	
9				9	
9					9

or

(b)

	9	9	10	14	12
13	4		6		3
14	5	9			
9			4	5	
9				9	
9					9

Both are basic feasible solutions with $5 + 5 - 1 = 9$ positive values, and both are optimal, with total cost 60, which is less than the optimal value in Example 5.1, which was 61.

The numbers in the diagonals are those out of the 9 added which were not needed for trans-shipment. The shadow costs are, in this case

u_1	u_2	u_3	u_4	u_5	v_1	v_2	v_3	v_4	v_5
0	−1	4	6	7	0	1	−4	−6	−7

There is, of course, no reason why the shadow costs should not be negative; the constraints of the transportation problem are equations, not inequalities.

The optimal plans are described in Fig. 5.3a and b.

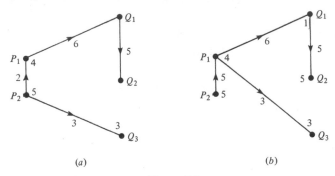

(a)   (b)

Figure 5.3

If we multiply solution (a) by 1/3 and solution (b) by 2/3, we obtain

	9	9	10	14	12
13	5		6		2
14	4	9			1
9			4	5	
9				9	
9					9

again with integer values, although this solution is not basic (not that this matters to the ships).

Transportation with capacity restrictions

If we think of ships sailing the seas, we do not envisage any restrictions on the numbers of ships on the same route, but this problem is a model for other distribution problems as well, so that restrictions on the capacities of channels may be relevant. Such 'capacitated' problems can also be solved by applying the methods which solve the transportation problem.

For instance, take again Example 5.1, but with the added restrictions $x_{1,2} \leqslant 3$, $x_{2,3} \leqslant 2$. We take our clue from the fact that a marginal row total or column total means implicitly a restriction on the values in that row or column. We write the capacity limits as totals of additional rows as well as columns, thus

	1	5	3	3	2
4	x_{11}	·	$x_{1,3}$	$x_{1,2}$	·
5	$x_{2,1}$	$x_{2,2}$	·	·	$x_{2,3}$
3	·	$x_{1,2}$	·	$y_{1,2}$	·
2	·	·	$x_{2,3}$	·	$y_{2,3}$

and we enter the $x_{i,j}$ as shown here. The original marginal totals are still valid, and the restrictions are active through the additional rows and columns. The $y_{i,j}$ values are entered, because we must make certain that the values which appear twice, e.g. $x_{1,2}$, will have the same value in each case. This is ensured by the implied equations $x_{1,2} + y_{1,2} = 3$ appearing twice, with $y_{1,2}$ written down only once.

Now we must fix the costs. Those of the $x_{i,j}$ which are merely restricted by the marginal totals are the same as before. A restricted variable appears twice, but its cost must be counted only once, so we attach the original cost when it appears in one of its positions, and 0 in its other position. The $y_{i,j}$ have cost 0, while the cells where an entry would not mean anything have a very high cost, say M. Therefore the cost matrix is now

4	M	7	5	M
7	10	M	M	8
M	0	M	0	M
M	M	0	M	0

The example will be solved by

	1	5	3	3	2	u_i
4			1	3		0
5	1	2			2	5
3		3		0		−5
2			2			−7
v_j	2	5	7	5	3	

$x_{i,j}$ (column header)

which means, in the original formulation

	1	5	3
4		3	1
5	1	2	2

We have now more positive entries than $m + n - 1 = 4$, but this is justified because we also have more constraints than before, because we have added limitations on two variables. We have therefore $4 + 2 = 6$ positive variables, two of them listed twice.

It turns out that the variables whose values had an upper bound imposed on them take precisely those upper bounds. From their values 4 and 3 in the solution of Example 5.1, they were reduced to 3 and to 2, respectively. However, this is not always the case. For instance, consider the following example.

Example 5.4

		b_j		
		2	4	3
a_i	3	8	1	10
	6	1	2	2

$c_{i,j}$

with optimal solution

	2	4	3
3		3	
6	2	1	3

cost 13

Now we restrict both $x_{1,2}$ and $x_{2,1}$ to be not larger than 1. If we reduce the present values of these variables to 1, we have

	2	4	3
3	1	1	1
6	1	3	2

cost 30

but the optimal solution is

	2	4	3
3	2	1	
6	0	3	3

cost 29

We can describe this result, which might seem surprising, in Simplex terms. The constraints of the transportation problem can be written, solving in terms of $x_{1,1}$ and $x_{1,3}$

$$x_{1,2} = 3 - x_{1,1} - x_{1,3} \qquad x_{2,2} = 1 + x_{1,1} + x_{1,3}$$
$$x_{2,3} = 3 \qquad - x_{1,3} \qquad x_{2,1} = 2 - x_{1,1}$$

i.e.

$$x_{1,1} + x_{1,3} \leqslant 3, \; x_{1,1} + x_{1,3} \geqslant -1, \; x_{1,3} \leqslant 3, \; x_{1,1} \leqslant 2$$
$$\text{all } x_{i,j} \geqslant 0$$

(of which the second and the third are redundant) and we minimize $13 + 8x_{1,1} + 9x_{1,3}$.

The optimal solution is $x_{1,1} = x_{1,3} = 0$, which means

$$x_{1,2} = 3, x_{2,2} = 1, \; x_{2,3} = 3, \; x_{2,1} = 2$$

as above. If we now also introduce

$$x_{1,2} = 3 - x_{1,1} - x_{1,3} \leqslant 1 \qquad x_{2,1} = 2 - x_{1,1} \leqslant 1$$

i.e.

$$x_{1,1} + x_{1,3} \geqslant 2, \ x_{1,1} \geqslant 1$$

then the optimal solution is $x_{1,1} = 2$, $x_{1,3} = 0$ (and not $x_{1,1} = 1$, $x_{1,3} = 1$), which means $x_{1,2} = 1$, $x_{2,2} = 3$, $x_{2,3} = 3$, $x_{2,1} = 0$, again as above (draw a diagram to see what happens!).

The transportation problem with restrictions can serve as a model if a range of availabilities were given rather than a fixed amount, while the requirements are fixed.

Example 5.5

Let $1 \leqslant a_1 \leqslant 7, \ 3 \leqslant a_2 \leqslant 5, \ 2 \leqslant a_3 \leqslant 9$

$$b_1 = 4, \ b_2 = 5$$

The largest possible $\Sigma_i \, a_i$ is 21; only 9 are required. We introduce a dummy requirement $21 - 9 = 12$, but restrict the variables in its column to the difference between the largest and the smallest admissible values of the a_i, thus

	4	5	12
7	$x_{1,1}$	$x_{1,2}$	$x_{1,3}$
5	$x_{2,1}$	$x_{2,2}$	$x_{2,3}$
9	$x_{3,1}$	$x_{3,2}$	$x_{3,3}$

with $x_{1,3} \leqslant 6$, $x_{2,3} \leqslant 2$, $x_{3,3} \leqslant 7$.

This ensures that the total of the values in the first two columns and in the first row, say, will not be less than 1 and not more than 7.

In Example 5.4 we had a case with a surprising answer. We add another example here, where the answer is also unexpected.

Example 5.6

a_1	a_2		b_1	b_2
6	1		4	3

$$c_{i,j}$$

10	3
2	5

with the optimal solution

$$x_{i,j}$$

	4	3	u_i
6	3	3	0
1	1		-8
v_j	10	3	

This solution has a cost of 41.

We decide now to send more from P_2 to Q_2, thus

a_1	a_2	b_1	b_2
6	2	4	4

with the same costs per unit. The optimal answer is now

$$x_{i,j}$$

	4	4	u_i	
6	2	4	0	
2	2		-8	
v_j	10	3		cost 36

The total cost has been reduced, although we send more now than before, on the same network, with unaltered unit costs.

This result can be made understandable through the concept of duality. We start with a transportation problem with constraints

$$\sum_j x_{i,j} = a_i, \quad \sum_i x_{i,j} = b_j$$

cost

$$\sum_i \sum_j c_{i,j} x_{i,j} = C$$

What we want to investigate is whether

$$\sum_j x_{i,j} \geqslant a_i, \quad \sum_i x_{i,j} \geqslant b_j$$

could possibly produce a smaller value of C.

The dual of the latter problem is maximize

$$\sum_i a_i u_i + \sum_j b_j v_j \; (= C)$$

subject to

$$u_i + v_j \leqslant c_{i,j}, \; u_i, v_j \geqslant 0 \; (\text{all } i, j)$$

If $u_i + v_j < 0$, then an increase of a_i, and an increase of b_j by the same amount, will decrease C. This is the situation in our example: $u_2 = v_2 = -5$ (but how far can this go on?).

A similar result would be obtained if the increase were spread over a number of a_is and b_js, when the sum of the corresponding u_is and v_js is negative.

As a further remark concerning the transportation problem we mention that the system of inequalities

$$\sum_{i=1}^n x_{i,j} \leqslant b_j, \; \sum_{j=1}^m x_{i,j} \leqslant a_i$$

i.e.

$$\sum_{i=1}^n x_{i,j} + y_j = b_j, \; \sum_{j=1}^m x_{i,j} + x_i = a_i$$

with

$$\sum_{i=1}^n a_i = \sum_{j=1}^m b_j$$

can also be put into the form of the transportation problem, by writing the table of variables

	b_1	$\ldots$	b_m	$\sum_{i=1}^n a_i$
a_1	$x_{1,1}$	$\ldots$	$x_{1,m}$	x_1
.	.		.	.
.	.		.	.
.	.		.	.
a_n	$x_{n,1}$	$\ldots$	$x_{n,m}$	x_n
$\sum_{j=1}^m b_j$	y_1	$\ldots$	y_m	z

where

$$z = \sum_{i=1}^{n} \sum_{j=1}^{m} x_{i,j}$$

The total of the row sums equals that of the column sums, and by the definition of z

$$\sum_{j=1}^{m} y_j + z = \sum_{i=1}^{n} x_i + z = \sum_{i=1}^{n} a_i = \sum_{j=1}^{m} b_j$$

Flow in networks

We shall now deal with a combinatorial problem which is also of linear programming type, but which can be solved by a method which makes direct use of its combinatorial features: the problem of constructing the largest flow in a network.

A set of points, some pairs of which are connected by links, is a *graph*. If numbers are attached to the links, then we call the graph a *network*.

Example 5.7

Consider Fig. 5.4 where the numbers attached to the directed links (arrows) give the largest flow allowed through that link in the direction of the arrow. We want to send the largest possible flow from the

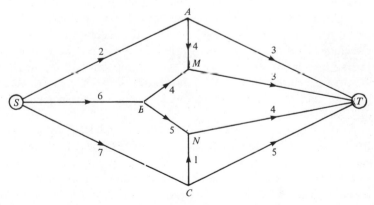

Figure 5.4

source S to the terminal T, taking into account the capacities of the links. This could be formulated as a linear programming problem, as follows.

Let $x_{i,j}$ be the flow from i to j. We wish to maximize

$$x_{SA} + x_{SB} + x_{SC}$$

subject to the capacity limitations and to the conditions that what goes in at any intermediate node, must go out again. These latter conditions are, in the present case

$$x_{SA} = x_{AT} + x_{AM}, x_{SB} = x_{BM} + x_{BN}, x_{SC} = x_{CN} + x_{CT},$$

$$x_{AM} + x_{BM} = x_{MT}, x_{BN} + x_{CN} = x_{NT}$$

It follows from these equations that

$$x_{SA} + x_{SB} + x_{SC} = x_{AT} + x_{AM} + x_{BM} + x_{BN} + x_{CN} + x_{CT}$$

$$= x_{AT} + x_{MT} + x_{NT} + x_{CT}$$

We could therefore say, equivalently, that we require the flow into T to be maximized. This is obvious from first principles. The same argument applies, of course, to any network: the total flow out of the source equals the total flow into the terminal.

The method which we want to use [5] begins by constructing some possible flow, and there is no difficulty about this: we can start with flow zero through all links. However, it is usually quite simple to start with some larger flow. We do this here, and we indicate the flow — which will nowhere exceed the allowed flow — by short arrows, to which the amount of flow is attached (the labels at the nodes are explained as we proceed). The total flow is 12. We try to find out if an increase of this flow is possible. We do this by attaching labels to the vertices. S is labelled (∞), to indicate that as far as S itself is concerned, any increase of a flow out of it is possible. We then attach the label (x, S) to those nodes into which more could be sent than the present flow from S, where x is the possible additional flow.

In our example the node A will not be labelled, since 2 is already the largest possible flow from S to A. B can be labelled $(1, S)$, and C can be labelled $(2, S)$ (see Fig. 5.5a).

If, from any labelled node V a further flow is possible into an adjacent one, we label the latter (y, V), where y is either the additional flow through the link from V, allowed by the capacity limitation, or the first item in the label of V (since this is the largest

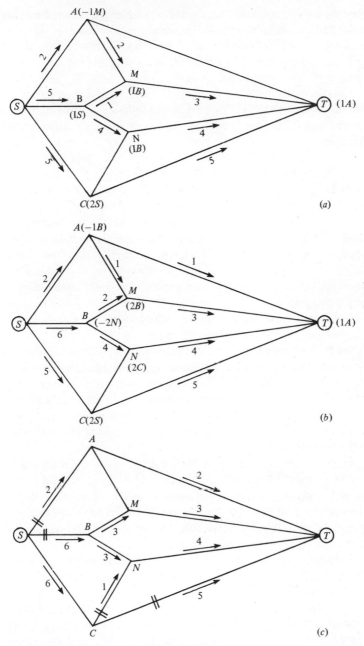

Figure 5.5a-c

additional flow that could be carried on) whichever is smaller. This is our first rule of labelling.

In our example, BM could take 3 more, but the label in B is $(1, S)$, and 1 is smaller than 3. Therefore M gets the label $(1, B)$. Similarly, concerning BN, N can be labelled $(1, B)$.

Now to the next labelled vertex, C. From here, we can go to N, but this is already labelled, so we ignore it. We can go from C to T, but the link CT is already full. No further labelling is possible by the first rule.

If we could, by this process, label T, by (y, R), say, then y more could be let into T than hitherto, and by going back as the second items in the labels indicate, y more could be got out of S to flow eventually into T. We could increase the total flow by y.

In the present example this was not possible by the first rule of labelling, but does this mean that we have already found the largest possible flow? It does not. The failure to label T may be a consequence of the pattern of the present flow. We must consider the possibility that by changing this pattern, we could then carry on with more success.

Re-arranging the pattern implies withdrawing some flow from a link and guiding it into another direction.

We shall withdraw a flow, or a portion of it, only into a node as yet unlabelled, and not more than can be replaced at the end of the link in question by an additional flow, which is indicated by its label. Accordingly, our second rule of labelling states that if there is a flow z from some unlabelled node into a labelled one, say from U to V, then label U by $(-t, V)$, where t is the smaller of z and of the first item in the label of V.

In our example, there is a flow of $z = 2$ from A (not labelled) into M [labelled $(1, B)$]. We have min$(2, 1) = 1$, and hence A is now labelled $(-1, M)$. The negative sign is there to show that we are withdrawing a flow. As far as the labelling rules are concerned, we ignore this sign. We shall send only 1 from A to M, and replace this at M by an additional flow of 1 from B.

There is no further opportunity in our example to use the second rule of labelling. We go now back to the first rule, and consider A, which is now labelled.

A has two adjacent nodes, M and T. M is already labelled, but T is not yet labelled. It can receive the label $(1, A)$. Now T has its label, and the total flow can be increased by 1. How this is done is given by the labels.

(1, A) means one more from A

(−1, M) at A means reduce the flow from A to M by 1

(1, B) at M means replace the loss of 1 by 1 from B

(1, S) at B means one more from S

The other flows are unaffected, even if other nodes, as for instance N, are labelled. The result is shown in Fig. 5.5b. The total flow is 12 + 1 = 13.

We label again, and can once more increase the flow. We go back through the nodes A, M, B, N, C, S (see Fig. 5.5c). The total flow is 13 + 1 = 14.

Label Fig. 5.5c. Only C can be labelled and no further flow can be found by our two labelling rules. Does this now mean that the maximal flow has been found? We shall prove that this is so.

To begin with, we introduce the concept of a 'cut'. It is a set of links, such that their removal severs any chain of links from S to T. For instance, the set of all links out of S is a cut, and so is the set of all links into T. Out of all cuts we are interested in that (or in those) cut(s), whose total link capacities are not larger than that of any other cut.

It is easily seen that no total flow can be larger than the total capacity of any cut. Otherwise, if we remove the links of the cut, some flow would remain, but there would not be any way for it to reach T from S. It follows that if we find a total flow which equals the total link capacity of some cut, then that flow is the largest possible, and this cut is minimal.

We shall now show that such a pair of flow and cut can be found, and that a maximal flow is obtained when the two rules of labelling the nodes do not produce a label for T.

We assert that, when no further labelling is possible, then a minimal cut consists of all links from a labelled node to an unlabelled node (in Fig. 5.5c, these are the links SA, SB, CN and CT, with a total capacity of 14). Such links always exist, because S is labelled and T is not, at this stage. Each such link contains a flow equal to its capacity, since otherwise its end-point could have been labelled. It is also clear that the set of the links mentioned forms a cut, because if we wanted to carry on towards T from any labelled node reached from S, we would have to use one of these links. Moreover, the sum of the capacities of these links must equal the total flow. The latter can not be larger, because no flow can be larger than any cut, but it cannot be smaller either, because each link of the cut carries as much as its capacity allows.

It follows that the links mentioned form a minimal cut, and that the flow which we have reached is maximal. We have thus proved the *Maximal-Flow/Minimal-Cut Theorem*, which asserts this equality.

We have derived the minimal cut from the maximal flow that we have found. There may exist other cuts with the same total capacity, for instance, in Fig. 5.5c the set (SA, MT, NT, CT), but this cut cannot be derived from a maximal flow in the manner shown. In fact, the maximal flow derived in Example 5.7 is unique.

If all capacities are integral, then the algorithm terminates, because we increase the flow at each stage by an integer value, and there is an integer upper bound to all possible total flows.

Dual networks

In Fig. 5.4 the links were drawn in such a way that no two of them intersected. If this is possible, we call the graph, or the network, 'planar'.

For a planar network of flows, with source S and terminal T, draw a line from S to T without intersecting any of the links of the network (see Fig. 5.6), and let its capacity be infinite. The plane is then partitioned into a number of continuous regions, one of them unbounded. In each region mark a point and connect two points in adjacent regions. To each of these latter links attach the number which is the capacity of the link which it crosses, and interpret this number as its 'length'. The network which we have thus constructed is the 'dual' of the original one. We want to find the shortest path between the two points in the regions separated by the added link of infinite capacity (U and V in Fig. 5.6).

The length of any path will, numerically, be the sum of the capacities of all those original links which the path intersects. The original links which any path intersects form a cut in the original network, and the length of the path equals the total capacity of the cut. If the latter is minimal, then we have found the shortest path.

As a consequence of the Max-Flow/Min-Cut Theorem we see that

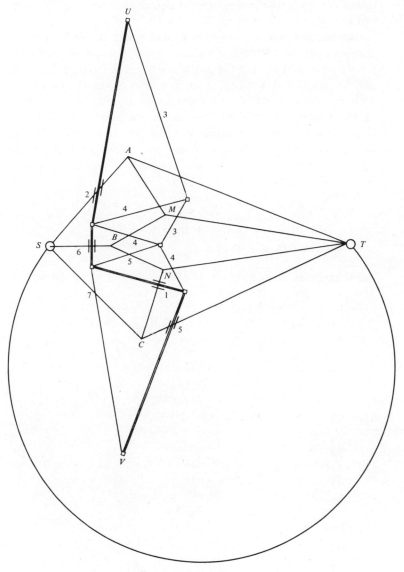

Figure 5.6

the maximal flow in a planar network equals the shortest path in its dual, between well defined points. Fig. 5.6 shows this for the network in Fig. 5.4.

Another method of solving the problem of Example 5.7 uses the Simplex algorithm. We take as variables the flows through chains, i.e. a succession of links. Let the chains from S to T be $D_j (j = 1, 2, \ldots)$ and let the flow through D_j be x_j. The links of the network are L_i with capacities $c_i (i = 1, 2, \ldots)$ and we write $a_{i,j} = 1$ if L_i is a portion of D_j, otherwise $a_{i,j} = 0$. We want to maximize the total flow $F = \Sigma_j x_j$, subject to the conditions that the sum of the flow through those chains which contain L_i must not exceed c_i. This can be written

$$\sum_j a_{i,j} x_j \leqslant c_i \text{ (all } i) \quad \text{or} \quad \sum_j a_{i,j} x_j + s_i = c_i$$

$$x_j \geqslant 0 \text{ (all } j), \quad s_i \geqslant 0 \text{ (all } i)$$

Now there may be many chains in a network, and we do not wish to determine all possible chains in advance but consider a chain only when we know that it leads to an improvement of the flow we have already reached. For the present example we list the subscripts of the links as follows:

link	i
SA	1
SB	2
SC	3
AT	4
AM	5
BM	6
BN	7
CN	8
CT	9
MT	10
NT	11

We start by taking the slack variables s_i as basic variables, and in the spirit of the Inverse Matrix Method we do not have any columns for the non-basic variables. Our first tableau is then

F	1						0
s_1	1						2
s_2		1					6
s_3		1					7
s_4		1					3
s_5			1				4
s_6			1				4
s_7				1			5
s_8				1			1
s_9				1			5
s_{10}					1		3
s_{11}						1	4

At this stage it is clear that the flow is 0, and can be increased by introducing any chain with a positive flow. Let us take the chain $D_1 = SAMT$, with

$$a_{3,1} = a_{5,1} = a_{10,1} = 1, \text{ all other } a_{i,j} = 0.$$

The corresponding column is

$$(-1, 1^*, 0, 0, 0, 1, 0, 0, 0, 0, 1, 0)'$$

(the prime indicating transposition, from the row vector to a column vector). Note that the value in the F-row is -1 for the initial column of any chain, because $F - \Sigma_j x_j = 0$.

By the rules of the Simplex Method, the pivot is in the row of s_1, because min $(2/1, 4/1, 3/1) = 2$. Hence the next tableau is

F	1	1					2
x_1	0	1					2
s_2	0	0	1				6
s_3	0	0	1				7
s_4	0	0	1				3
s_5	0	−1		1			2
s_6	0	0		1			4
s_7	0	0			1		5
s_8	0	0			1		1
s_9	0	0			1		5
s_{10}	0	−1				1	1
s_{11}	0	0				1	4

(the empty spaces contain 0). We have reached a flow of 2. In the spirit of the Inverse Matrix Method we say that we have multiplied the first tableau (the identity matrix, and the column of capacities) by an elementary matrix E_1, derived from the column of D_1.

We must now find out whether the complete tableau, with the columns of all variables, has a negative value in the F-row. If this is the case, then we can increase F further by a Simplex iteration.

Let the F-row of a tableau be $(+1, f_1, f_2, \ldots, f_n)$, with all f_i non-negative, and let the column of some chain be $(-1, d_1, \ldots, d_n)'$ with all d_i non-negative. After transformation, the top value of this column will be $(f_1 d_1 + \cdots + f_n d_n - 1)$ and this can only be negative, namely, -1, if $d_i = 0$ whenever $f_i > 0$. In the present case this means that the new chain must not contain the link SA, because $f_1 = 1$.

Let us choose such a chain without SA, say $D_2 = SBMT$

$$a_{2,2} = a_{6,2} = a_{10,2} = 1$$

with column

$$(-1, 0, 1, 0, 0, 0, 1, 0, 0, 0, 1^*, 0)'$$

This column remains unchanged if we pre-multiply it by E_1, because E_1 differs from the identity matrix only in the column of SA, and the new chain has been chosen so that it does not contain this link.

The pivot is in the row of s_{10}, the new elementary matrix differs from the identity matrix in the column of MT, and we obtain

F	1	0								1	0	3
x_1	1									0	0	2
s_2	1	1								-1	0	5
s_3	0		1							0	0	7
s_4	0			1						0	0	3
s_5	-1				1					0	0	2
s_6	1					1				-1	0	3
s_7	0						1			0	0	5
s_8	0							1		0	0	1
s_9	0								1	0	0	5
x_2	-1									1	0	1
s_{11}	0									0	1	4

Now we are looking for a chain which does not contain the link MT (only this column has a 1 in the F-row, apart from that for F itself). If it does not contain SA either, then no transformation of its vector will be required at this stage (because all columns apart from that of

SA and MT are unit vectors). So let us take $D_3 = SBNT$

$$a_{2,3} = a_{7,3} = a_{11,3} = 1$$

with column

$$(-1, 0, 1, 0, 0, 0, 0, 1, 0, 0, 0, 1*)'$$

The pivot is the last component, and the next tableau is

F	1	0								1	1	7
x_1		1								0	0	2
s_2		1	1							−1	−1	1
s_3		0		1						0	0	7
s_4		0			1					0	0	3
s_5		−1				1				0	0	2
s_6		1					1			−1	0	3
s_7		0						1		0	−1	1
s_8		0							1	0	0	1
s_9		0								1	0	0	5
x_2		−1								1	0	1
x_3		0								0	1	4

Now it is convenient to choose a chain without SA, MT and NT, so let us take $D_4 = SCT$

$$a_{3,4} = a_{9,4} = 1$$

with column

$$(-1, 0, 0, 1, 0, 0, 0, 0, 0, 1*, 0, 0)'$$

leading to

F	1	0								1	1	1	12
x_1		1								0	0	0	2
s_2		1	1							0	−1	−1	1
s_3		0		1						1	0	0	2
s_4		0			1					0	0	0	3
s_5		−1				1				0	0	0	2
s_6		1					1			0	−1	0	3
s_7		0						1		0	0	−1	1
s_8		0							1	0	0	0	1
x_4		0								1	0	0	5
x_2		−1								0	1	0	1
x_3		0								0	0	1	4

$D_5 = SAT$ ($a_{1,5} = a_{4,5} = 1$) is the only chain not containing CT, MT

or NT, with column

$$(-1, 1, 0, 0, 1, 0, 0, 0, 0, 0, 0, 0)'$$

This must be transformed before we continue; it transforms into

$$(-1, 1, 1^*, 0, 1, -1, 1, 0, 0, 0, -1, 0)'$$

and we obtain the tableau

F	1	1	1							1	0	0	13
x_1	0	0	-1							0	1	1	1
x_5	0	1	1							0	-1	-1	1
s_3	0	0	0	1						-1	0	0	2
s_4	0	-1	-1		1					0	1	1	2
s_5	0	0	1			1				0	-1	-1	3
s_6	0	0	-1				1			0	0	1	2
s_7	0	0	0					1		0	0	-1	1
s_8	0	0	0						1	0	0	0	1
x_4	0	0	0							1	0	0	5
x_2	0	0	1							0	0	-1	2
x_3	0	0	0							0	0	1	4

We are now looking for a chain without SA, SB, CT. Such a chain is only $D_6 = SCNT$ ($a_{3,5} = a_{8,5} = a_{11,5} = 1$)

with column

$$(-1, 0, 0, 1, 0, 0, 0, 0, 1, 0, 0, 1)'$$

transformed into

$$(-1, 1^*, -1, 1, 1, -1, 1, -1, 1, 0, -1, 1)'$$

leading to

F	1	1	0							1	1	1	14
x_6		1	1							0	1	1	1
x_5		0	1							0	-1	0	2
s_3		-1	1	1						-1	-1	-1	1
s_4		-1	0		1					0	0	0	1
s_5		1	0			1				0	0	0	4
s_6		-1	0				1			0	-1	0	1
s_7		1	-1					1		0	1	0	2
s_8		0	0						1	0	0	0	0
x_4		0	0							1	0	0	5
x_2		1	0							0	1	0	3
x_3		-1	1							0	-1	0	3

This is the final tableau, because there is no chain without SA, CT, MT, NT. The answer is, of course, the same as that found earlier by another method.

At each stage we had to find a chain which did not include certain specified links. This is often possible by inspection. Otherwise, for finding such a chain, we could assume that each link of the network has capacity 1, that all those links which we wish to exclude are already used to capacity, and then find a flow, of 1, from S to T by the labelling method, which is in this case very simple indeed. Alternatively, we might drop those unwanted links from the network altogether, and find a flow from S to T, if possible.

The transportation problem — revisited

We return now to the transportation problem and mention a method for its solution in which the labelling method of the maximum flow algorithm, or a method equivalent to it, is being used, as a sub-routine.

Given availabilities a_i at points P_i, and requirements b_j at points Q_j, with $\Sigma_i a_i = \Sigma_j b_j$, we can illustrate the redistribution of goods by the flow through a network as shown in Fig. 5.7. We have arrows from points P_i to points Q_j without any restriction on their capacities. We have also introduced a master source P and a master terminal Q. From P we have links a_i to P_i, with capacities a_i, respectively. This ensures that not more than a_i can leave P_i. Similarly, the links from

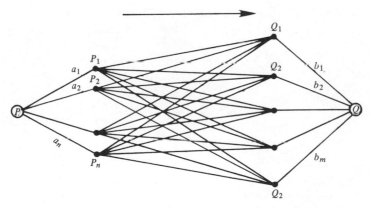

Figure 5.7

Q_j to Q have capacities b_j. This ensures that not more than b_j will arrive at Q_j. Since the total of the a_i equals the total of the b_j, we can also be certain that precisely a_i will leave P_i, and precisely b_j will arrive at Q_j.

This time it is not a question of how much can be moved from P to Q. This is, of course, $\Sigma_i\, a_i$, but this can be done in various ways, and we want to find the way which minimizes $\Sigma_i\, \Sigma_j\, c_{i,j}x_{i,j}$, where $c_{i,j}$ is the known cost of sending one unit from P_i to Q_j, and $x_{i,j}(\geqslant 0)$ is the amount sent.

We illustrate the method by solving Example 5.1 again. Its network is as shown in Fig. 5.8. In linear programming terms, we have minimize

$$4x_{1,1} + 5x_{1,2} + 7x_{1,3} + 7x_{2,1} + 10x_{2,2} + 8x_{2,3}$$

subject to

$$x_{1,1} + x_{1,2} + x_{1,3} = 4,\ x_{2,1} + x_{2,2} + x_{2,3} = 5$$

$$x_{1,1} + x_{2,1} = 1,\ x_{1,2} + x_{2,2} = 5,\ x_{1,3} + x_{2,3} = 3$$

all $x_{i,j} \geqslant 0$

The dual of this problem is maximize

$$4u_1 + 5u_2 + v_1 + 5v_2 + 3v_3$$

subject to

$$u_1 + v_1 \leqslant 4,\ u_1 + v_2 \leqslant 5,\ u_1 + v_3 \leqslant 7$$

$$u_2 + v_1 \leqslant 7,\ u_2 + v_2 \leqslant 10,\ u_2 + v_3 \leqslant 8$$

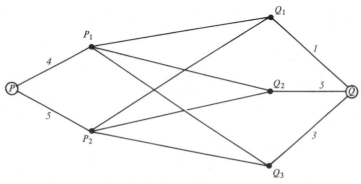

Figure 5.8

The u_i and v_j may be positive, zero or negative. A solution of the constraints of the dual problem can be found by making all $v_j = 0$, and letting u_1 and u_2 have the largest values then possible. In the present case, this means $u_1 = 4$, $u_2 = 7$. We attach these values to the rows and columns of the table of the transportation problem.

	1	5	3	u_i
4	4	5	7	4
5	7	10	8	7
v_j	0	0	0	

We know that in the optimal solution we shall find $u_i + v_j \leqslant c_{i,j}$ for those links which do not contain a flow, and $u_i + v_j = c_{i,j}$ for those which do. Therefore, we try to send as much as possible through those links for which the equation holds at present. These links are $P_1 Q_1$ and $P_2 Q_1$ and they require flows in PP_1, PP_2 and in $Q_1 Q$ as well.

Let us try to pass as much as possible from P to Q with the given capacities of PP_1, PP_2, and $Q_1 Q$. If we could send $\Sigma_{i=1}^2 a_i = 9$ — which we can plainly not do, as yet — then we would have solved the problem.

To find the largest flow from P to Q we use the labelling method, starting with some possible flow, e.g. 1, through the chain $P \rightarrow P_1 \rightarrow Q_1 \rightarrow Q$ (see Fig. 5.9). Instead of doing the labelling on the graph, we shall do it on the table of the transportation problem. Translated into these terms, the rules are as follows.

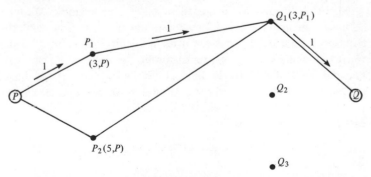

Figure 5.9

Put a circle round those $c_{i,j}$ values which equal $u_i + v_j$. Choose some possible flow $x_{i,j}$ in the corresponding link(s) and mark the corresponding circle(s) by that flow. Now start the labelling of rows and columns.

If the total flow in the circles of row i is smaller by r_i than a_i, label the row $(r_i, 0)$. This corresponds to a label on one of the P_i. If a row is labelled, and there is a circle in that row, label the column of this circle, if it is still unlabelled, (r_i, i). This corresponds to a label on one of the Q_j.

	1	5	3		
4	④'	5	7	4	$(3, 0)$
5	⑦	10	8	7	$(5, 0)$
	0	0	0		
	$(3, 1)$				

If in a column j thus labelled there is a circle with a flow attached to it, label the row of this circle, if it is still unlabelled, (s_i, j), where s_i is the smaller of r_i in the column's label, and the flow. This corresponds to labelling by the second labelling method explained earlier. In the present example such a situation does not arise, because both rows are already labelled.

Continue labelling as far as possible. If in this manner a column is labelled in which the flow is still smaller than b_j, then this corresponds to labelling the master sink Q, and an increase of the total flow is possible. We call this event a 'breakthrough'.

No breakthrough has occurred so far in our example. We must therefore change the u_i and v_j to obtain a larger flow, and this requires that new links must be made available by making $c_{i,j}$ equal to $u_i + v_j$, while $u_i + v_j \leqslant c_{i,j}$ remains valid for all links. We can make more links available by looking at labelled rows and unlabelled columns and adding to the u_is of the rows the largest amount possible, say t, without making $c_{i,j}$ smaller than u_i. In the present case t will be the smallest of

$$5 - 4 \qquad 7 - 4$$
$$10 - 7 \qquad 8 - 7$$

i.e. $t = 1$. Also, we shall not lose any circle with a flow in it if we deduce t from v_j in a labelled column.

In our example, we have then a new graph, and a table with more circles. We continue with this example, and show at each stage the diagram which is equivalent to the table, for the purpose of illustration.

After adding 1 to u_1 and to u_2, and subtracting 1 from v_1

	1	5	3		
4	④^1	⑤	7	5	(3, 0)
5	⑦	10	⑧	8	
	−1	0	0		Q is labelled. Breakthrough
	(3,1)	(3,1)			(see Fig. 5.10a)

We have already obtained a breakthrough and therefore we do not continue labelling the second row by (5, 0). We add 3 to the link (P_1, Q_2).

	1	5	3		
4	④^1	⑤^3	7	5	
5	⑦	10	⑧	8	(5, 0)
	−1	0	0		Q is labelled. Breakthrough
	(5, 2)		(5, 2)		(see Fig. 5.10b)

Another breakthrough; add 3 to (P_2, Q_3)

	1	5	3		
4	④^1	⑤^3	7	5	(1, 1)
5	⑦	10	⑧^3	8	(2, 0)
	−1	0	0		Q is labelled. Breakthrough
	(2, 2)	(1, 1)	(2, 2)		(see Fig. 5.10c)

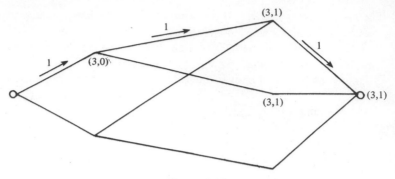

Figure 5.10a

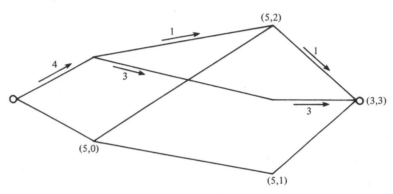

Figure 5.10b

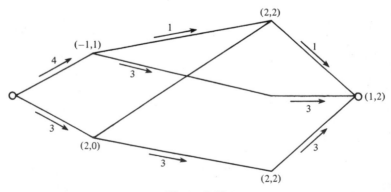

Figure 5.10c

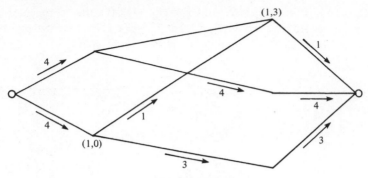

Figure 5.10d

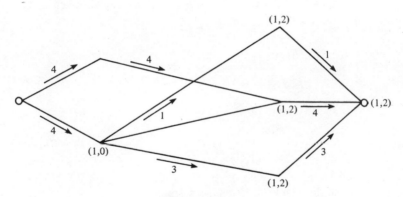

Figure 5.10e

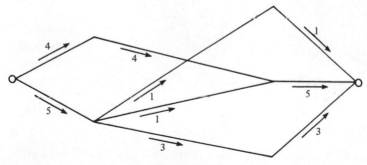

Figure 5.10f

113

Breakthrough in column 2. Add 1 to (P_1, Q_2). But then compensating changes are required in (P_1, Q_1) and (P_2, Q_1). They are indicated by the labels. See the diagram, with labels $(-1, 1)$ and $(1, 1)$.

	1	5	3		
4	④	⑤⁴	7	5	
5	⑦¹	10	⑧³	8	(1, 0)
	−1	0	0		(see Fig. 5.10d)
	(1, 2)		(1, 2)		

No breakthrough. $t = 10 - 8 = 2$. Add 2 to u_2 and subtract 2 from v_2. This gives a new diagram.

	1	5	3		
4	4	⑤⁴	7	5	
5	⑦	⑩	⑧³	10	(1, 0)
	−3	0	−2		Q is labelled. Breakthrough.
	(1, 2)	(1, 2)	(1, 2)		(see Fig. 5.10e)

This breakthrough leads to

	1	5	3		
4	4	5	7	5	
5	7	10	8	10	
	−3	0	−2		No labels!
					(see Fig. 5.10f)

which is clearly the final solution.

Problems

5.1. 5 units of a commodity are available at A_1 and 3 units at A_2. 2 units are required at B_1, 2 units at B_2 and 4 units at B_3. The costs of transport between any two of the places are given in the following table:

	A_1	A_2	B_1	B_2	B_3
A_1	0	2	5	7	7
A_2	2	0	7	3	8
B_1	5	7	0	1	3
B_2	7	3	1	0	1
B_3	7	8	3	1	0

Find the cheapest way of distributing the commodity (a) with trans-shipment, (b) without trans-shipment.

5.2. Availabilities, requirements, and costs are as in Problem 5.1, but route A_2B_2 cannot take more than 4 units. Find the cheapest way of distribution, with trans-shipment.

5.3. In the network given in the following figure, with the capacities of the links indicated, find the largest flow from S to T and determine the cut of smallest total capacity.

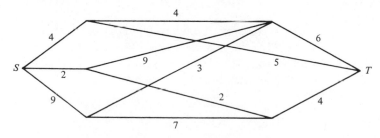

Figure to problem 5.3

CHAPTER 6

Integer programming

We have seen in Chapter 5 that if we have a transportation problem with integer requirements and integer availabilities, then the solution will also be expressed in integers. This is, of course, necessary if the requirements and availabilities refer to indivisible items such as, for instance, ships.

There are other problems which demand the answer to be given in integers to make sense. However, we cannot always rely on obtaining integer values from a solution by the Simplex Method, even if the formulation of a realistic problem makes this necessary. Consider, for instance, the following example.

Example 6.1
A railway management runs trains with 4 first class and 4 second class carriages, and also trains with 2 first class and 6 second class carriages.

The income from these two types of trains is, in proportion, 5 to 3. There are altogether 45 first class and 60 second class carriages available simultaneously. How many trains of each type should be run at the same time, to maximize the total income?

If we denote the number of trains of the first type by x_1, and that of the second type by x_2, then we have the constraints

$$4x_1 + 2x_2 \leqslant 45, \quad 4x_1 + 6x_2 \leqslant 60$$

x_1 as well as x_2 must be non-negative, and we wish to maximize $5x_1 + 3x_2$.

By the Simplex Method we obtain

	x_1	x_2			x_3	x_2	
B	-5	-3	0	B	5/4	$-1/2$	225/4
x_3	4*	2	45	x_1	1/4	1/2	45/4
x_4	4	6	60	x_4	-1	4*	15

	x_3	x_4	
B	9/8	1/8	465/8
x_1	3/8	−1/8	75/8
x_2	−1/4	1/4	15/4

We have now solved the problem as formulated, but we want to have the answer in integers.

We consider two types of integer programming problems: *pure integer programming*, when all variables are required to take values, and *mixed integer programming*, when this requirement refers only to specified variables. In either case, we shall consider linear constraints, and a linear objective function.

First, we deal with pure integer linear programming, and we start with a method due to Gomory [7]. This method attacks the problem, to begin with, by using the Simplex or the Dual Simplex Method. If all variables are already integer in the solution, then we have found the answer to our problem. Otherwise, there will be at least one variable whose value is not an integer. Denote it by x.

Let there be t non-basic variables $x_1, \ldots, x_t$, and let the row of the objective function, or of a basic variable in the Simplex Tableau be

	x_1	x_2	...	x_t	
x	z_1	z_2	...	z_t	z_0

Let $z_i = N_i + f_i$ for $i = 0, 1, \ldots, t$, where N_i is the largest integer not exceeding z_i, so that $f_i \geqslant 0$ ($i = 1, \ldots, t$) and $f_0 > 0$ (if f_0 were 0, then we would not be concerned, at this stage, with x). At least one of the f_i must be positive, for us to continue. If none were positive, then no integer solution could exist.

We have

$$x + f_1 x_1 + \cdots + f_t x_t + N_1 x_1 + \cdots + N_t x_t = N_0 + f_0 \qquad (6.1)$$

or

$$f_1 x_1 + \cdots + f_t x_t - f_0 = N_0 - x - N_1 x_1 - \cdots - N_t x_t \qquad (6.2)$$

Define

$$s = f_1 x_1 + \cdots + f_t x_t - f_0$$

Because s equals the right hand side of Equation (6.2) it is required to be an integer; by its definition, it is not smaller than the negative fraction $-f_0$. Hence it must be a non-negative integer, like all other variables.

Introduce s into the final Simplex tableau in a new row, as follows

$$x_1 \quad \ldots \quad x_t$$

$$s \quad -f_1 \quad \ldots \quad -f_t \qquad -f_0$$

The tableau is still dual feasible, because the row of its objective function is that of the final Simplex tableau. We apply the Dual Simplex Method, thus making s non-basic at the next step.

By introducing the new constraint, we did not exclude any integer solution from the feasible region, because the components of such a solution will make s, as defined, a non-negative integer. However, we do cut off portions of that region. For this reason we call the method a 'cutting plane' method.

If, after introducing s and solving the enlarged problem, we have still a non-integer variable left, then we continue by introducing yet another variable, and so on. Whenever one of the newly introduced variables becomes basic again, we can drop it with its row. Hence there will be never more than $n + 1$ of these variables in our tableaus. Eventually all remaining variables must be integer and non-negative.

Because the method requires the introduction of new variables, we shall want to know whether it terminates after a finite number of steps. We do not enter more deeply into an investigation of this point, but we quote from Gomory's original publication: 'A rule of choice of row which can be shown to bring the process to an end in a finite number of steps . . . will be given'.

We illustrate the method by solving Example 6.1. The final Simplex tableau reads

	x_3	x_4	
B	9/8	1/8	465/8
x_1	3/8	−1/8	75/8
x_2	−1/4	1/4	15/4

and, taking the first row as a source, we add the row

| s_1 | −1/8 | −1/8* | −1/8 |

which transforms into

	x_3	s_1			s_2	s_1	
B	1	1	58	B	2	1	57
x_1	1/2	−1	19/2	x_1	1	−1	9
x_2	−1/2	2	7/2	x_2	−1	2	4
x_4	1	−8	1	x_4	2	−8	0
s_2	−1/2*	0	−1/2	x_3	−2	0	1

We could have obtained the final values of x_1 and x_2 by rounding to the nearest integer, but this is a coincidence and could not be relied on in all cases. At any rate, such a rounding of B would have been incorrect.

In terms of the problem, the railway management should run nine trains of the first type (using 36 first class and 36 second class carriages), and four trains of the second type (using 8 first class and 24 second class carriages) which leaves one first class carriage unused. This ensures the largest total income.

Fig. 6.1 follows the computations. Without the requirement of integrality, the largest income would be at (75/8, 15/4). The constraint

$$s_1 - x_3/8 - x_4/8 = -1/8$$

which means

$$s_1 - (45 - 4x_1 - 2x_2)/8 - (60 - 4x_1 - 6x_2)/8 = -1/8$$

(i) (75/8, 15/4)

(ii) (19/2, 7/2)

(iii) (9,4)

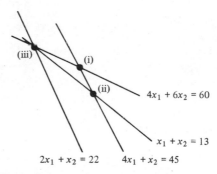

Figure 6.1

or

$$s_1 - 13 + x_1 + x_2 = 0$$

i.e.

$$x_1 + x_2 \leqslant 13$$

cuts off a portion of the feasible region, and

$$s_2 - x_3/2 = -1/2$$

which means

$$s_2 - (45 - 4x_1 - 2x_2)/2 = -1/2$$

or

$$s_2 - 22 + 2x_1 + x_2 = 0$$

i.e.

$$2x_1 + x_2 \leqslant 22$$

cuts off another portion.

We turn now to mixed integer programming. We look again at the final Simplex tableau, and in particular at a variable which was specified as one whose value should be, but is not yet, integral. Let it be the variable x.

We denote the non-basic variables in such a way that the first k values in the row of x are non-negative, while those remaining are negative. Thus

$$x_1 \quad \ldots \quad x_k \; x_{k+1} \quad \ldots \quad x_t$$

$$x \qquad z_1 \quad \ldots \quad z_k \; z_{k+1} \quad \ldots \quad z_t \qquad z_0$$

with $z_i (i = 1, \ldots, k) \geqslant 0$ and $z_i (i = k + 1, \ldots, t) < 0$.

Let $z_0 = N + f$, with N an integer and $0 < f < 1$. We denote

$$\sum_{i=1}^{k} z_i x_i$$

by P, and

$$\sum_{i=k+1}^{t} z_i x_i$$

by Q. We also note that $P \geqslant 0$ and $Q \leqslant 0$. We shall write g for $f/(1 - f)$ and note that $g > 0$. With this notation, we have

$$P + Q = N - x + f$$

Consider the two cases (i) $P + Q \geqslant 0$ and   (ii) $P + Q < 0$.

(i) Because $N - x$ must be an integer, $P + Q$ will be f, or $f + 1$, or $f + 2, \ldots$, and so $f \leqslant P + Q \leqslant P < P - gQ$ (since $Q \leqslant 0, g > 0$).

(ii) $P + Q$ is $f - 1$, or $f - 2, \ldots$, and so $f - 1 \geqslant P + Q \geqslant Q$, $1 - f \leqslant -Q, f = g(1 - f) \leqslant -gQ \leqslant P - gQ$.

We see that in either case $f \leqslant P - gQ$. If we now introduce, as a new variable

$$s = P - gQ - f$$

then $s \geqslant 0$ can be added as a further constraint. It will not exclude any solutions of the original constraint which contain x with an integral value.

The value of s in the tableau into which we introduce it will be $-f$, which is negative. We carry on with the Dual Simplex Method and if the next tableau contains an unwanted fractional value again, then we continue the procedure. It can be shown that the procedure terminates after a finite number of steps, if certain conditions concerning the feasible region are satisfied and if the objective function is also required to have an integral value.

Example 6.2

We take again the objective function and the constraints of Example 6.1, but this time we demand only that x_2 be an integer.

The Simplex Method leads again to

	x_3	x_4	
B	9/8	1/8	465/8
x_1	3/8	−1/8	75/8
x_2	−1/4	1/4	15/4

Considering x_2, we have $f = 3/4, g = 3$ and $P = x_4/4, Q = -x_3/4$. The new constraint is introduced by the row

s	−3/4	−1/4*	−3/4

and we obtain, after one iteration

	x_3	s	
B	3/4	1/2	231/4
x_1	3/4	−1/2	39/4
x_2	−1	1	3
x_4	3	−4	3

If, alternatively, we specify x_1 and start again from the final Simplex tableau above, then considering x_1, we have $f = 3/8$, $g = 3/5$, and $P = 3x_3/8$, $Q = -x_3/8$, so that the new row is

| s | −3/8 | −3/40* | −3/8 |

which gives

	x_3	s	
B	1/2	5/3	115/2
x_1	1	−5/3	10
x_2	−3/2	10/3	5/2
x_4	5	−40/3	5

The final optimal values of the objective function are 57 when both x_1 and x_2 are specified; 57 1/2 (57 3/4) when only x_2 (only x_1) is specified, and 58 1/8 when no integrality condition is imposed.

Branch and bound algorithm

We mention a computing method [11] which is much favoured for solving integer linear programming problems and illustrate it by using the formulation of Example 6.1 again.

We have solved this example by first ignoring the requirement of integrality, and we obtained at this stage $x_1 = 9\ 3/8$, $x_2 = 3\ 3/4$, $B = 58\ 1/8$. x_1 as well as x_2 contained fractions. Let us first concentrate on x_1, and try the adjacent integer values, namely

(a) $x_1 \leqslant 9$

(b) $x_2 \geqslant 10$

The problem is the same as before, with one further constraint, respectively. The solution of the original problem will be implied in one of the new problems. The solutions of the latter are found (e.g. by the Simplex Method)

(a) $x_1 = 9, x_2 = 4, x_3 = 1, x_4 = 0$

$B = 57$

(b) $x_1 = 10, x_2 = 2\frac{1}{2}, x_3 = 0, x_4 = 5$

$B = 57\frac{1}{2}$

As it happens, with $x_1 \leqslant 9$ we have already obtained a solution with integral values, while this is not so with $x_1 \geqslant 10$ (we could have known that the optimal values of x_1 would be 9 or 10, respectively, by noticing that the feasible region is convex. Relying on this, we could have solved the two problems (a) and (b) by making x_1 equal to one of these values). We have a higher value of B in (b), but when we introduce the integrality condition on x_2, the value of B might be smaller than 57. We split (b) again into two parts, adding to the original constraints

$$x_1 \geqslant 10, x_2 = 2$$

The answer is $B = 56$, less than 57 which we already know how to obtain.

$$x_1 \geqslant 10, x_2 = 3$$

This is obviously not feasible.

In other cases we might have to branch out for more variables. At any stage the best value so far obtained, with integer variables, will be a bound below which we need not go; when we obtain a lower value, we stop branching.

It is clear that this method can be used equally well for pure and for mixed integer problems. There exist more sophisticated versions of the branch and bound algorithm, in particular when the variables can only have the values 0 or 1, but we are content to have explained here the underlying principle.

Applications of integer programming

We mention a few applications of integer programming, to show the great variety of possible uses of this branch of linear programming.

1. Suppose that we wish to maximize the value of a non-linear function $f(x)$, and that we are satisfied to replace the function by a broken line function, consisting of straight line segments between points $(a_i, f(a_i))$, $(i = 1, \ldots, n)$. Any point on the broken line function can be represented by the co-ordinates

$$x = \sum_{i=0}^{n} \lambda_i a_i \quad f(x) = \sum_{i=0}^{m} \lambda_i f(a_i)$$

$$\sum_{i=0}^{n} \lambda_i = 1 \quad \lambda_i \geqslant 0 \; (i = 0, \ldots, n)$$

provided that only one of the λ_i, or two adjacent λ_i are positive (not zero).

This proviso can be enforced by

$$\lambda_0 \leqslant \delta_0$$

$$\lambda_1 \leqslant \delta_0 + \delta_1$$

$$\lambda_2 \leqslant \delta_1 + \delta_2$$

$$. \quad . \quad .$$
$$. \quad . \quad .$$
$$. \quad . \quad .$$

$$\lambda_i \leqslant \delta_{i-1} + \delta_i$$

$$. \quad . \quad .$$
$$. \quad . \quad .$$
$$. \quad . \quad .$$

$$\lambda_{n-1} \leqslant \delta_{n-2} + \delta_{n-1}$$

$$\lambda_n \leqslant \delta_{n-1}$$

with $\displaystyle\sum_{i=1}^{n-1} \delta_i = 1$, and each δ_i equals either 0 or 1.

2. Let x be subject to the alternative $x = 0$, or $\geqslant 10$, while $x \leqslant 10^t$. This can be written

$$x = 10\delta \geqslant 0, \quad -x + 10^t \delta \geqslant 0$$

where $\delta = 0$ or 1. Indeed, if $\delta = 1$, then $x - 10 \geqslant 0, x \leqslant 10^t$ and if $\delta = 0$, then $x \geqslant 0, -x \geqslant 0$, i.e. $x = 0$.

3. Let $x_i \leqslant N_i (i = 1, \ldots, n)$ and not more than k of the x_i can be positive. The others must be zero.

This can be written

$$x_i \geqslant 0, x_i \leqslant \delta_i N_i, \quad \sum_{i=1}^{n} \delta_i \leqslant k$$

each $\delta_i = 0$ or 1.

4. We want to formulate $x_1 \neq x_2$, where x_1 and x_2 are positive integers and it is known that each is less than n or equal to n. We write this

$$x_1 - x_2 \geqslant 1 - \delta n$$

$$x_2 - x_1 \geqslant 1 + \delta n - n$$

Now if $\delta = 0$, then

$$x_1 - x_2 \geqslant 1$$

$$x_2 - x_1 \geqslant 1 - n \text{ (redundant)}$$

and if $\delta = 1$, then

$$x_1 - x_2 \geqslant 1 - n \text{ (redundant)}$$

$$x_2 - x_1 \geqslant 1$$

In either case x_1 and x_2 cannot be equal.

5. We want to colour a map with the smallest number of colours, but no two adjacent countries must have the same colour. Let the countries be $i = 1, 2, \ldots, n$ and the colours available $j = 1, 2, \ldots, n$ (we might not need so many, but certainly we shall not need more).

If country i has colour j, then let $x_{i,j} = 1$, otherwise $x_{i,j} = 0$. All countries must have some colour, hence $\Sigma_j x_{i,j} = 1$ for all i. If i_1 and i_2 are two adjacent countries, then

$$x_{i_1,j} + x_{i_2,j} \leqslant 1$$

for all j. Introduce the integer variable y_j, so that

$$y_j \geqslant \sum_{i=1}^{n} x_{i,j}/n$$

and minimize $\Sigma_j y_j$. We know that $\Sigma_i x_{i,j} \leqslant n$ (the number of countries with colour j, for all j), so that $\Sigma_i x_{i,j}/n$ is either zero, or positive, but not larger than 1. Hence the integer y_j, when minimized, is either zero (if j is not used at all), or 1 (when j is used). It follows that $\min \Sigma_j y_j$ is the smallest number of colours needed.

The celebrated *'four-colour' theorem*, recently proved but conjectured for a long time, states that in no map will more than four colours be required. There can be maps where less than four colours would not do.

6. We want to buy x_i units of goods $G_i (i = 1, \ldots, n)$ and each unit of G_i costs c_i. Also, when we order any positive amount of G_i, we incur a 'fixed charge' f_i (positive).

Moreover, the x_i are subject to

$$\sum_{i=1}^{n} a_{i,j} x_j = b_j (j = 1, \ldots, m)$$

These constraints must be satisfied at least cost, remembering the fixed charges.

If we have upper limits u_i for the x_i (which is a realistic assumption) then we can formulate this problem as follows. Minimize

$$\sum_{i=1}^{n} (\delta_i f_i + c_i x_i)$$

subject to

$$\sum_{i=1}^{n} a_{i,j} x_i = b_j \text{ (all } j) \tag{6.3}$$

$$0 \leqslant x_i \leqslant \delta_i u_i \text{ (all } i) \tag{6.4}$$

$$\delta = 0 \text{ or } 1 \quad \text{(all } i)$$

Because $f_i > 0$, each δ_i will be as small as possible. δ_i will be 0 if $x_i = 0$, as a consequence of Equation (6.4). The objective function will then not contain f_i. Otherwise δ_i will be unity, f_i appears in the objective function, and $x_i \leqslant u_i$ does not add any new information.

7. The knapsack problem

We want to go on a hike and would like to take with us various items with weights w_i but we cannot carry a heavier total load than W.

We assess therefore the value of each item, v_i, say, and want to choose the items, within the total weight limitation, so that the total value of those items which we take with us is largest. We also assume that the values of the items are additive.

This problem can be formulated as taking x_i items of type i, so that

$$\sum_i v_i x_i$$

is maximized, subject to

$$\sum_i w_i x_i \leqslant W$$

all x_i non-negative and integer.

Column generation

We exhibit now a method of dealing with large linear programming problems which makes use of the knapsack problem as a sub-routine.

When we were dealing with the Decomposition algorithm, we saw that it was not necessary to know the columns of all the non-basic variables in the Simplex tableau. We constructed only some of those columns, equal in number to the number of the basic variables, and then generated new columns, for the iterations, when this could be shown to be useful. We shall now apply this idea to a case in which we can make use of integer linear programming.

Paper mills produce paper of given width and any required length. Customers require paper of various length and width, but for some purpose it is not necessary that the total length required of a given width should be supplied in a continuous strip. The manufacturer will have to cut the total width of the paper as produced, and at the edges some wastage will occur. We want to see how this wastage could be minimized.

Assume that the width of the paper, as produced by the manufacturer, is 200 cm, and that the following orders have been received:

length	150 cm	of width	100 cm
	80		60
	100		35

The width of 200 can be partitioned in various ways into portions of width 100, 60 or 35. For instance, it can be cut into twice 100 with no wastage or into once 100, once 60, and once 35 (with a wastage of 5) or into once 100 and twice 35 (with a wastage of 30) and in many other ways as well.

There are many possibilities and we want to avoid working them all out. We try to consider only those cutting patterns which might be used when making the total wastage as small as possible.

Let us call the numbers with which width 100, 60 and 35 can be accommodated within 200, respectively, a_1, a_2 and a_3. In the three examples above we have $a_1 = 2$, $a_2 = a_3 = 0$, or $a_1 = a_2 = a_3 = 1$, or $a_1 = 1, a_2 = 0, a_3 = 2$. They must satisfy

$$100a_1 + 60a_2 + 35a_3 \leqslant 200$$

If we used only those partitions mentioned, we could satisfy the orders received by taking length x_1, x_2 and x_3, respectively, with width 200 partitioned in those ways, and we would have to solve

$$2x_1 + x_2 + x_3 = 150$$
$$x_2 \qquad = 80$$
$$x_2 + 2x_3 = 100$$

The solution of this system is

$$x_1 = 30, x_2 = 80, x_3 = 10$$

The total length of the paper to be cut is 120, and the pattern of cuts is shown in Fig. 6.2a.

The width of 35 would be supplied in one strip of length 80 and two strips of length 10 each, adding up to 100 as required. The width of 100 would be supplied in two strips of length 30, one of length 80, and one of length 10, and the width of 60 in one strip of 80.

This pattern of cutting produces a wastage of

$$80 \times 5 + 10 \times 30 = 700.$$

This is, of course, the same as

$$200(x_1 + x_2 + x_3)$$

less the paper ordered, namely

$$200 \times 120 - (150 \times 100 + 80 \times 60 + 100 \times 35).$$

We can therefore say that we want to make $x_1 + x_2 + x_3$ as small as possible. In these terms, and taking into account the length of x_i of all possible partitions, our problem can be formulated as: minimize

$$C = \sum_i x_i$$

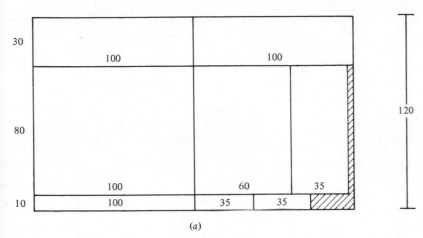

(a)

Figure 6.2a

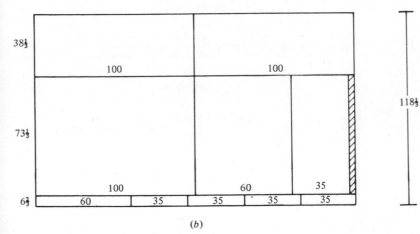

(b)

Figure 6.2b

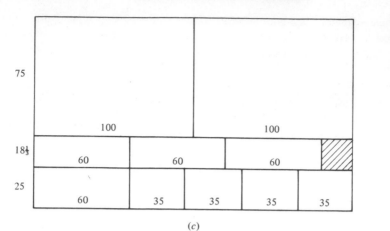

(c)

Figure 6.2c

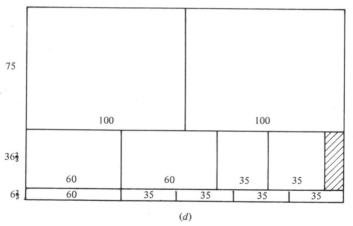

(d)

Figure 6.2d

subject to

$$\sum_i a_{1i}x_i \geqslant 150$$

$$\sum_i a_{2i}x_i \geqslant 80$$

$$\sum_i a_{3i}x_i \geqslant 100$$

$$x_i \geqslant 0 \text{ (all } i)$$

where (a_{1i}, a_{2i}, a_{3i}) defines the ith partition of 200, and must therefore satisfy

$$100a_{1i} + 60a_{2i} + 35a_{3i} \leqslant 200 \text{ (all } i)$$

We have written the restraints as inequalities rather than as equations, because the widths and requirements may be such that equations have no non-negative solutions. (For instance, if the total width were 100, and if the required length of width 60 were 100, and that of width 35 were 10.)

We describe now our procedure in terms of the Inverse Matrix Method. We start with the tableau

	C	x_1	x_2	x_3	
C	1	-1	-1	-1	0
x_{104}	0	-2	-1	-1	-150
x_{105}	0	0	-1	0	-80
x_{106}	0	0	-1	-2	-100

We have solved this system of equations above for x_1, x_2 and x_3. We could get the same result after a number of iterations. In one single step, this means that we can pre-multiply the tableau by E, say, the inverse of the matrix consisting of the columns of C, x_1, x_2, x_3 above. We have

$$E = \begin{pmatrix} 1 & -1/2 & -1/4 & -1/4 \\ 0 & -1/2 & 1/4 & 1/4 \\ 0 & 0 & -1 & 0 \\ 0 & 0 & 1/2 & -1/2 \end{pmatrix}$$

which gives

	C	x_1	x_2	x_3	
C	1	0	0	0	120
x_1	0	1	0	0	30
x_2	0	0	1	0	80
x_3	0	0	0	1	10

However, we do not know if this gives the smallest possible wastage.

The original tableau, if complete, would have contained columns

$$\begin{pmatrix} -1 \\ -a_{1,i} \\ -a_{2,i} \\ -a_{3,i} \end{pmatrix}$$

and after pre-multiplication, the new tableau contains the column

$$-1 + a_{1,i}/2 + a_{2,i}/4 + a_{3,i}/4$$
$$a_{1,i}/2 - a_{2,i}/4 - a_{3,i}/4$$
$$a_{2,i}$$
$$-a_{2,i}/2 + a_{3,i}/2$$

It is, in fact, only the first row which we need. We want to know if, for any of the various values of i, this value is positive. If there is one such i, then we make the corresponding variable (or one of them) basic, to reduce C. Equivalently, we ask whether the largest of those values is positive, i.e. we ask for the maximum of

$$a_1/2 + a_2/4 + a_3/4 - 1$$

subject to

$$100a_1 + 60a_2 + 35a_3 \leqslant 200$$

where a_1, a_2 and a_3 must have, of course, non-negative integer values.

This is an integer linear programming problem with one single constraint: a knapsack problem. The solution is

$$a_1 = 0, a_2 = 1, a_3 = 4$$

and

$$a_1/2 + a_2/4 - 1 \text{ positive}$$

We therefore introduce a new variable, say x_4, and a column which was originally

$$\begin{pmatrix} -1 \\ 0 \\ -1 \\ -4 \end{pmatrix}$$

and which, pre-multiplied by E, will be

$$\begin{pmatrix} 1/4 \\ -5/4 \\ 1 \\ 3/2* \end{pmatrix} \quad \text{Comparing with} \quad \begin{matrix} 120 \\ 30 \\ 80 \\ 10 \end{matrix}$$

we find that the pivot is $3/2$, in the last row. We therefore pre-multiply E by the elementary matrix

$$\begin{pmatrix} 1 & 0 & 0 & -1/6 \\ 0 & 1 & 0 & 5/6 \\ 0 & 0 & 1 & -2/3 \\ 0 & 0 & 0 & 2/3 \end{pmatrix}$$

and obtain

	C	x_1	x_2	x_4	
C	1	1/2	1/3	1/6	118 1/3
x_1	0	1/2	-2/3	1/6	38 1/3
x_2	0	0	4/3	-1/3	73 1/3
x_4	0	0	-1/3	1/3	6 2/3

(see Fig. 6.2b). Continuing in the same spirit, we maximize

$$a_1/2 + a_2/3 + a_3/6 - 1$$

subject to

$$100a_1 + 60a_2 + 35a_3 \leqslant 200$$

all a_i integer $\geqslant 0$. The maximum is 0 for

$$\begin{pmatrix} a_1 \\ a_2 \\ a_3 \end{pmatrix} = \begin{pmatrix} 0 \\ 3 \\ 0 \end{pmatrix} \text{ or } \begin{pmatrix} 0 \\ 2 \\ 2 \end{pmatrix}$$

so that alternatives to our last result, with the same value of C, can be found. They are, if we attach the variables x_5 and x_6 to the two new possibilities

$$x_1 = 75, \quad x_5 = 18 \ 1/3, \quad x_4 = 25, \quad C = 118 \ 1/3$$

see Fig. 6.2c, and

$$x_1 = 75, \ x_6 = 36 \ 2/3, \ x_4 = 6 \ 2/3, \ C = 118 \ 1/3.$$

see Fig. 6.2d.

It will be noticed that x_1 and x_4 refer to patterns which do not lead to any wastage, and they are part of all three optimal solutions. However, this is not necessarily true in other combinations. We remark, also, that it is usual in problems of this type for multiple solutions to occur.

Problems

6.1. Solve Problem 2.3 with the further condition that all variables must have integer values.

6.2. Solve Problems 3.1(a) and (b) with the further condition that all variables must have integer values.

CHAPTER 7

Linear programming under uncertainty

Until now, when we have been dealing with linear programming, we have always assumed that the constants in the objective function, and those in the constraints, were precisely known. In many practical applications this is not so. We shall now consider cases where the constant terms in the constraints are not precisely known; we know only their probability distributions.

Let it be required to minimize

$$c_1 x_1 + \cdots + c_n x_n$$

subject to

$$a_{j,1} x_1 + \cdots + a_{j,n} x_n = b_j \, (j = 1, \ldots, m)$$

$$x_i \geqslant 0 \, (i = 1, \ldots, n)$$

and let it be also known that b_j takes one of a finite number of discrete values $b_{j,k} \, (k = 1, 2, \ldots)$ with probability $p_{j,k}$.

It is then not possible to demand that the variables take values so that the left hand sides of all constraints equal the right hand side precisely, whatever the right hand sides might be. When any values $x_1, \ldots, x_n$ have been determined, the difference

$$b_j - a_{j,1} x_1 - \cdots - a_{j,n} x_n$$

will be a random variable. If b_j has the value $b_{j,k}$, the difference may be positive, negative or zero, and we can write

$$a_{j,1} x_1 + \cdots + a_{j,n} x_n + y_{j,k} - z_{j,k} = b_{j,k}$$

$$y_{j,k} \geqslant 0, z_{j,k} \geqslant 0$$

for $j = 1, \ldots, m$ and $k = 1, 2, \ldots$ Of course, $y_{j,k}$ and $z_{j,k}$ must not be both positive. We return to this point later.

We argue now that we choose the x_i at a first stage, and that at a second stage we have to pay penalties for any discrepancies between the actual values of b_j and $\Sigma_i \, a_{j,i} x_i$. We shall then want to make the expected value of the sum of all penalties as small as possible, together with minimizing $\Sigma_i \, c_i x_i$, the original objective function.

We assume that the penalty for a positive $y_{j,k}$ is $f_j y_{j,k}$, and for a positive $z_{j,k}$ it is $g_j z_{j,k}$, with $f_j \geqslant 0$ and $g_j \geqslant 0$. Then our problem becomes minimize

$$\sum_{i=1}^{n} c_i x_i + f_1 \sum_k p_{1,k} y_{1,k} + \cdots + f_m \sum_k p_{m,k} y_{m,k}$$

$$+ g_1 \sum_k p_{1,k} z_{1,k} + \cdots + g_m \sum_k p_{m,k} z_{m,k}$$

subject to

$$a_{j,1} x_1 + \cdots + a_{j,n} x_n + y_{j,k} - z_{j,k} = b_{j,k} \quad (j = 1, \ldots, m)$$
$$(k = 1, 2, \ldots)$$

$$x_i, y_{j,k}, z_{j,k} \geqslant 0 \text{ (all } i, j, k)$$

We are thus led to an enlarged linear programming problem.

We must deal with an apparent difficulty, that is with the suspected possibility that it may turn out that some $y_{j,k}$ and $z_{j,k}$ with the same subscripts are positive simultaneously, which would not make any realistic sense. However, this cannot happen. The objective function contains the terms

$$p_{j,k}(f_j y_{j,k} + g_j z_{j,k})$$

and for any value of $y_{j,k} - z_{j,k}$ (positive or negative) that term will be minimized by making either $y_{j,k}$, or $z_{j,k}$ zero, or both, since the f_j and g_j are non-negative.

Example 7.1
Let $x_1 + 2x_2$ be maximized, subject to $x_1 + x_2 = b$, where b takes the value 5 or 7, each with probability $1/2$.

If b turns out to be 5, then any deviation of $x_1 + x_2$ from 5 (positive or negative) incurs a penalty of 2 per unit, while if $b = 7$, the penalty is 4 per unit. This means

$$B = x_1 + 2x_2 - 2(\tfrac{1}{2} y_1 + \tfrac{1}{2} z_1) - 4(\tfrac{1}{2} y_2 + \tfrac{1}{2} z_2)$$

subject to

$$x_1 + x_2 + y_1 - z_1 = 5$$

$$x_1 + x_2 + y_2 - z_2 = 7$$

$$x_1, x_2, y_1, y_2, z_1, z_2 \geqslant 0$$

We start with

	x_1	x_2	z_1	z_2	
B	-4	-5	2	4	-19
y_1	1	1	-1	0	5
y_2	1	1	0	-1	7

and obtain, eventually, $x_2 = 7$, $z_1 = 2$, all other variables equal to zero, and $B = 12$.

It should be noted that if the penalties are low, compared with the coefficients of the objective function, then it might be worth while to increase some variables without bounds, and to incur thereby the penalties to be expected, since these might be more than compensated for by the increase of the objective function.

We deal now with an approach to the problems involving uncertainty which differs from that which we have just described. Instead of requiring given constraints to be satisfied precisely, we shall now consider constraints with random elements and demand that the variables be chosen so that the constraints hold with given probabilities.

Take the constraint $ax = a_1x_1 + a_2x_2 + \cdots + a_nx_n \geqslant b$, where b has the distribution given by prob $(b \leqslant z) = F(z)$, and the condition

$$\text{prob}(ax \geqslant b) \geqslant \alpha$$

This requirement is equivalent to

$$ax \geqslant B_\alpha \tag{7.1}$$

where B_α is such that $F(B_\alpha) = \alpha$.

Indeed, if Expression (7.1) holds, then ax will not be less than any b not larger than B_α, and the probability of b being such is α. Conversely, if Expression (7.1) does not hold, then $ax \geqslant b$ has a smaller probability than α.

In the same way we can show that

$$\text{prob } (ax \leqslant b) \leqslant \alpha \quad \text{is equivalent to } ax \geqslant B_{1-\alpha}$$

$$\text{prob } (ax \geqslant b) \leqslant \alpha \quad \text{is equivalent to } ax \leqslant B_{\alpha}$$

and that

$$\text{prob } (ax \leqslant b) \geqslant \alpha \quad \text{is equivalent to } ax \leqslant B_{1-\alpha}$$

Example 7.2

Minimize

$$20x_1 + 10x_2$$

subject to

$$\text{prob } (3x_1 + x_2 \geqslant b_1) \geqslant 1/3$$

$$\text{prob } (4x_1 + 3x_2 \geqslant b_2) \geqslant 1/3$$

$$\text{prob } (x_1 + 2x_2 \geqslant b_3) \geqslant 1/2$$

$$x_1, x_2 \geqslant 0$$

where b_1, b_2 and b_3 have rectangular distributions, b_1 between 2 and 5, b_2 between 2 and 14, and b_3 between 0 and 4. Now

$$\text{prob } (b_1 \leqslant 3) = 1/3$$

$$\text{prob } (b_2 \leqslant 6) = 1/3$$

$$\text{prob } (b_3 \leqslant 2) = 1/2$$

so that the equivalent constraints are

$$3x_1 + x_2 \geqslant 3$$

$$4x_1 + 3x_2 \geqslant 6$$

$$x_1 + 2x_2 \geqslant 2$$

Thus our problem reduces to Example 1.2.

More complicated problems, e.g. where the a_i are probabilistic, and other extensions as well as an extensive bibliography are contained in [13].

Problems

7.1 Maximize

$$x_1 + x_2$$

subject to

$$x_1 + 2x_2 = b, x_1, x_2 \geqslant 0$$

where b takes the value 5 with probability 1/2 and the value 7 with probability 1/2. Any deviation of $x_1 + 2x_2$ from 5 incurs a penalty of 2 per unit, and any deviation from 7, incurs a penalty of 4 per unit.

7.2. Maximize

$$5x_1 + 6x_2$$

subject to

$$\text{prob} (3x_1 + 4x_2 \leqslant b_1) \geqslant 1/3$$

$$\text{prob} (2x_1 + x_2 \leqslant b_2) \geqslant 1/3$$

$$x_1, x_2 \geqslant 0$$

where $b_1(b_2)$ in rectangularly distributed between 15 and 21 (between 4 and 10).

Answers to problems

Chapter 1

1.1. (0, 0)   (3.5, 0)   (0, 4.5)   (2, 3)

Chapter 2

2.1(a) Last tableau

	x_4	x_3	
B	2/5	7/5	28
x_2	−3/5	2/5	3
x_1	4/5	−1/5	2

$x_1 = 2, x_2 = 3, B = 28$

(b) Last tableau

	x_1	x_3	
C	−19/2	−3/2	−27
x_2	3/4	1/4	4.5
x_4	5/4	−1/4	2.5

$x_1 = 0, x_2 = 0, C = −27$

2.2. $x_1 = 0, x_2 = 4.5$, and also $x_1 = 2, x_2 = 3$: objective function 36

2.3. Last tableaus

	x_1	x_3			x_1	x_4	
C	−19/2	−3/2	−27	C	−17	−3	−27
x_2	3/4	1/4	4.5	x_3	−5	−2	0
				x_2	2	1/2	4.5

Both define the same point, namely $x_1 = 0, x_2 = 4.5$

2.4. Introducing parameters, maximize

$$3.5\lambda_2 + 36\lambda_3 + 26\lambda_4 + 5x_3$$

subject to

$$3.5\lambda_2 + 18\lambda_3 + 14\lambda_4 + 5x_3 \leqslant 7$$

$$\lambda_1 + \lambda_2 + \lambda_3 + \lambda_4 = 1$$

$$\lambda_i \geqslant 0, x_3 \geqslant 0$$

Answer: $\lambda_1 = 11/18$, $\lambda_3 = 7/18$, i.e. $x_1 = 0$, $x_2 = 7/4$, $x_3 = 0$, objective function 14

2.5. Final tableaus

$t \leqslant 6$

	x_1	x_2		
B	$-5+t$	$-6+t$	0	
x_3	3	4	18	
x_4	2	1	7	$(0, 0)$

$2 \leqslant t \leqslant 6$

	x_1	x_3		
B	$-1/2+t/4$	$3/2-t/4$	$27-9t/2$	
x_2	$3/4$	$1/4$	$9/2$	
x_4	$5/4$	$-1/4$	$5/2$	$(0, 9/2)$

$t \leqslant 2$

	x_4	x_3	
B	$2/5-t/5$	$7/5-t/5$	$28-5t$
x_2	$-3/5$	$2/5$	3
x_1	$4/5$	$-1/5$	2

Note: when $t = 2$, we obtain the answer to Problem 2.1, with its objective function halved

2.6 Last tableau

	x_4	x_2	
B	1	−2	1
x_3	1	−1	2
x_1	1	−1	1

i.e. B can increase without bounds

2.7.

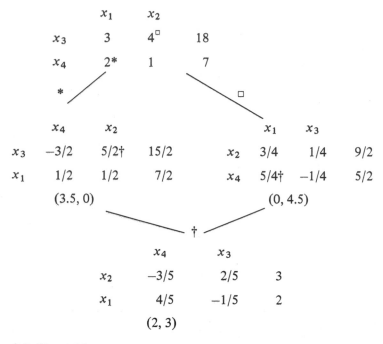

	x_1	x_2	
x_3	3	$4^\square$	18
x_4	2*	1	7

	x_4	x_2	
x_3	−3/2	5/2†	15/2
x_1	1/2	1/2	7/2

(3.5, 0)

	x_1	x_3	
x_2	3/4	1/4	9/2
x_4	5/4†	−1/4	5/2

(0, 4.5)

	x_4	x_3	
x_2	−3/5	2/5	3
x_1	4/5	−1/5	2

(2, 3)

2.8. First tableau

	x_1	x_2	x_3	
u_1	−1/5	0	0	0
u_2	1/10	−2/5	0	0
s_1	0	1/5	−1/5	0
s_2	1	1	1	1

where x_i are the proportion in g_i, u_1 and u_2 are the recruitments into g_1 and g_2, respectively

Final tableaus

	x_1			u_2			u_1	
u_1	−0.2	0	u_1	2/3	2/15	u_2	1.5	0.2
u_2	0.3	0.2	x_1	10/3	2/3	x_1	−5	0
x_2	0.5	0.5	x_2	−5/3	1/6	x_2	2.5	0.5
x_3	0.5	0.5	x_3	−5/3	1/6	x_3	2.5	0.5

Chapter 3

3.1(a) Minimize $18y_3 + 7y_4$ subject to

$$3y_3 + 2y_4 \geqslant 5$$
$$4y_3 + y_4 \geqslant 6$$
$$y_3, y_4 \geqslant 0$$

last tableau

	y_2	y_1	
C	−3	−2	28
y_4	3/5	−4/5	2/5
y_3	−2/5	1/5	7/5

(b) Maximize $-18y_3 - 7y_4 - Mz$ subject to

$$-3y_3 - 2y_4 + y_1 = 5$$
$$4y_3 + y_4 - y_2 + z = 6$$
$$y_j, z \geqslant 0$$

last tableau

	y_4	y_2	
B	5/2	9/2	−27
y_1	−5/4	−3/4	19/2
y_3	1/4	−1/4	3/2

3.2. The problem is minimize $x_1 + x_2$ subject to

$$-x_1 + x_2 - x_3 = 1$$
$$x_1 - x_2 - x_4 = 1$$
$$x_i \geqslant 0$$

Last tableau

	x_1	x_2	x_3	x_4	
C	-1	-1	$-M$	$-M$	$2M$
z_1	-1	1	-1	0	1
z_2	1	-1	0	-1	1

i.e. the problem has no feasible region (remember that its dual had an infinite objective function!)

Chapter 4

4.1. Pay-off table

	12	14	24
2	-1	7	2
4	7	-3	-2

A should choose 2, or 4, in proportions $3:1$
B should choose 12, or 24, in proportions $1:2$
A ought to pay an entry fee of 1

4.2. Pay-off table

	(1, 1)	(1, 2)	(2, 1)	(2, 2)
(1, 1)	0	2	-3	0
(1, 2)	-2	0	0	3
(2, 1)	3	0	0	-4
(2, 2)	0	-3	4	0

Two basic solutions: $(0, 4/7, 3/7, 0)$ and $(0, 3/5, 2/5, 0)$

Chapter 5

5.1(a) Optimal distribution

	A_2	B_1	B_2	B_3	
A_1	3	2			
A_2			6		
B_2				4	cost 38

(b) Optimal distribution

	B_1	B_2	B_3	
A_1	2		3	
A_2		2	1	cost 45

5.2. Optimal distributions

	A_2	B_1	B_2	B_3
A_1	1	4		
A_2			4	
B_1			2	
B_2				4

and

	A_2	B_1	B_2	B_3
A_1	1	2		2
A_2			4	
B_2				2

cost 40

5.3.
The cut consists of SA, SB, CD, ET. Total capacity 13

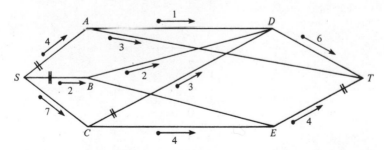

Figure to answer of problem 5.3

Chapter 6

6.1. Final tableaus

	x_1	s	
C	-5	-6	-24
x_2	0	1	4
x_4	3	-2	1
x_3	3	-4	2

and

	x_1	s	
C	-17	-6	-24
x_3	-5	-4	2
x_2	2	1	4
x_4	0	-2	1

They give the same point

6.2(a) Final tableau

	s_1	s_2	
C	-3	-3	32
y_4	3	-3	2
y_3	$-4/3$	1	1
y_2	1	1	0
y_1	2	-3	2

(b) Final tableau

	s_1	s_2	
B	4	3	-32
y_1	1	-3	12
y_3	-1	1	1
y_2	-2	1	0
y_4	2	-3	2

Chapter 7

7.1. Last tableau

	x_2	x_1	y_2	z_2	
B	1	2	2	2	5
x_1	2	0	1	-1	7
z_1	0	-1	1	-1	2

7.2. Equivalent constraints

$$3x_1 + 4x_2 \leqslant 19, 2x_1 + x_2 \leqslant 8$$

Answer: $x_1 = 13/5, x_2 = 14/5, B = 149/5$

References

[1] Charnes, A. (1952), Optimality and degeneracy. *Econometrica*, **20**, 160–70.

[2] Dantzig, G. B. (1951), Maximization of a linear function of variables subject to linear inequalities, in *Activity Analysis of Production and Allocation*, (ed. T. C. Koopmans) J. Wiley & Sons, New York, pp. 339–47.

[3] Easterfield, T. E. (1946), A combinatorial algorithm. *J. London Math. Soc.*, **21**, 219–26.

[4] Farkas, J. (1902), Über die Theorie der einfachen Ungleichungen. *J.f. reine und angew. Math.*, **124**, 1–24.

[5] Ford, L. R., jun. and Fulkerson, D. R. (1957), A simple algorithm for finding maximal network flows and an application to the Hitchcock problem. *Can. J. Math.*, **9**, 210–18.

[6] Ford, L. R., jun. and Fulkerson, D. R. (1956), Solving the transportation problem. *Man. Science*, **3**, 24–32.

[7] Gomory, R. E. (1958), Essentials of an algorithm for integer solutions to linear programs. *Bull. Amer. Math. Soc.*, **64**, 275–78.

[8] Hall, P. (1935), On representation of sub-sets. *J. London Math. Soc.*, **10**, 26–30.

[9] Hitchcock, F. L. (1941), The distribution of a product from several sources to numerous localities. *J. Math. and Phys.*, **20**, 224–30.

[10] Kuhn, H. W. and Tucker, A. W. (eds.) (1956), *Linear Inequalities and Related Systems. Annals of Math. Study no. 38*, Princeton University Press, Preface xi–xiii.

[11] Land, A. H. and Doig, A. G. (1960), An automatic method of solving discrete programming problems. *Econometrica*, **28**, 497–520.

[12] Tucker, A. W. (1956), Dual systems of homogeneous linear relations, in *Linear Inequalities and Related Systems* (eds. H. W. Kuhn and A. W. Tucker), Princeton University Press, pp. 3–18.

[13] Vajda, S. (1972), *Probabilistic Programming*, Academic Press.

Index